D1151182

A Year in Muswell Hill

A Year in Muswell Hill

by

Pierre LaPoste

Translated from the French

by

Geneviève Tomlinson

Paperback ISBN 1 903970 77 6

**Published
by**

Central Publishing Limited
Royd Street Offices
Milnsbridge
Huddersfield
West Yorkshire
HD3 4QY

www.centralpublishing.co.uk

To my good friend, neighbour and Literary Agent R. M. Sharples, without whose help and encouragement, these memoirs would not have been completed.

Pierre LaPoste
Muswell Hill
England

A Year in Muswell Hill

JANUARY

T HE YEAR BEGAN with a *petit déjeuner*, or breakfast, in what the English call a "greasy spoon" café. For very good reason. As I stared down at my plate of fried eggs, fried bacon, fried bread, fried sausage and, as far as I could tell, fried baked beans, all sitting glumly in a pool of rapidly congealing, supposedly virgin olive oil - (but which, by its colour, would appear to have lost its virginity many fry-ups ago) - I could not help but reflect upon the train of events that had brought me from my home in the little village of Ménerbes in the South of France, to *Sid's Diner* in North London's Muswell Hill Broadway, at ten o'clock in the morning, on a cold and overcast New Year's Day.

By profession I am a journalist - a food, wine and travel writer for the French national newspaper *Le Courrier de Paris* and my job was to write a regular column on the wines, restaurants and hotels of Provence, from Aix-en-Provence to Apt in the Lubéron, as well as covering the coastal holiday resorts from Marseilles to Monaco. I say that *was* my job because of an unfortunate series of happenings that culminated in a telephone call from *Le Courrier's* travel editor instructing me to leave Provence for London immediately - as a temporary replacement for their long-time London correspondent. It appeared that after a long and laborious food-and-wine tasting session in one of London's leading roof-terrace restaurants, he had become rather indisposed and had very properly decided to throw up over the roof-top parapet rather than over the restaurant's Maitre D'.

Unfortunately, as he leaned over the parapet, he seemed to have had a sudden rush of blood (or perhaps *Château Lafite '81*) to the head and he had lost his balance. As the travel editor had said on the telephone: 'Antoine Didier has fallen in the line of duty - in a manner of speaking.'

It seemed that the unfortunate *bon viveur* had ended up at the bottom of a road-works trench in London's Park Lane, many metres below. At the time, the road-works foreman had peered down to the bottom of the trench and with typically English pragmatic *sang froid*, had reportedly said:

'It's hardly worth digging him out.'

I had viewed the prospect of a move to England with mixed feelings. I enjoyed living in Ménerbes and working from home, even though my Parisian-born wife had long decided that village life was not only boring, with little or nothing to do, that our neighbours were equally boring and, significantly, that I was the most boring of all. To be fair, she did have a point. The trouble was, because of my profession, even though we shared a house in the centre of Ménerbes, we didn't see very much of each other - she spending most of her time on shopping trips to Aix-en-Provence and taking the

TGV to Paris to visit her (she claimed) aged mother. It has to be said that after the first few months of marriage, it soon became clear that we had little in common. I had - and still have - a love of fine wines and fine food. She was completely the opposite, constantly fighting to maintain her Parisian-slim figure on a diet of goat's cheese, organic lettuce and *Perrier* - while I was required to travel the Lubéron eating enormous meals at the many little restaurants in Lacoste, Bonnieux, Oppède and Goult.

Thus I cannot honestly say that her decision to remain in Paris with her aged mother and, as it transpired, a wealthy Parisian plastic surgeon (who would presumably keep her in the shape to which she would like to become accustomed), came as much of a surprise. Though I was, of course, shocked and appalled by my wife's duplicity, I also cannot honestly say that her abrupt departure caused me much grief, as I was now able to invite the plumply-pretty Michelle from the local *pâtisserie* to stay the night, rather than us having to conduct our affair as furtively as we had over the past eighteen months.

Even so, at the time of the telephone call from *Le Courrier's* travel editor, I was beginning to have second thoughts about living permanently in Ménerbes. There were two reasons for this, the first being the way in which the village had changed since the arrival, some years ago, of an obscure English writer (whose name escapes me) who had written a book about the joys of moving from England to Provence. Though I also cannot recall the title of the book, it recounted the author's experiences while spending a year in Provence and was very successful, even though I failed to recognise the village as described in the book or the characters who supposedly populated it. But the book did seem to strike a chord with all those who wistfully envied the author's obviously halcyon existence and induced many curious tourists to visit the area - Ménerbes in particular - who then filled the local restaurants, jammed the streets with their *Hertz* hire cars and sent the local prices almost as high as *Mont Ventoux.*

Even though the surrounding land was swiftly converted into temporary car parks, it still became almost impossible for the residents - including myself - to park their automobiles reasonably close to their homes. At the height of the season, on looking up from my computer, I rarely failed to see a succession of squinting German, Japanese, English, Italian and even French faces, their noses pressed against the downstairs front windows as they peered into a genuine Ménerbes living room occupied by a genuine Ménerbes resident who was disappointingly working at his computer instead of wolfing down *patés* of rabbit, boar, duck, and thrush, followed by pork *terrine*, wild mushrooms and *saucissons* spotted with peppercorns - which, according to the book, every Ménerbes resident was traditionally required to consume on a daily basis. And it was beginning to irritate me.

The second reason was that the aforesaid plumply-pretty Michelle from the local *pâtisserie* was beginning to show signs of growing more plump and less pretty, due to the increasing number of free cream pastries she consumed every day. More importantly, in the absence of my wife, she was also showing signs of wanting to move in to my house on a permanent basis, which would have spoilt everything. I was enjoying my new-found freedom and needed my own space. Furthermore, I had no wish to marry for a second time, as Michelle obviously wanted me to - which, of course, was the sole reason why I continued to refuse to give my wife an immediate divorce -

despite her admitted and quite shameless adultery.

So after my telephone conversation with the travel editor, I had no hesitation in informing Michelle that I had no choice but to go to London and that our relationship would have to be put on hold until my return, secure in the knowledge that once I was out of the way, it wouldn't be long before Monsieur Gaston Lafarge from the nearby funeral parlour - who I knew had a penchant for pink, plump, uninhibited young women - would be knocking at the *pâtisserie* back door with a bunch of flowers borrowed from the cemetery and an invitation to a candle-lit liaison in the Chapel of Rest.

The following day, I changed the locks on *Chez Moi*, as a precaution against my wife, hearing that the house was unoccupied, attempting to gain entry and spirit away anything of value. I then shuttered the windows, informed the local *gendarmerie* of my extended absence and boarded the *TGV* from Aix to Lille, where I changed trains. It was late on New Year's Eve when I finally stepped off the *Eurostar* at London's Waterloo Station and took a taxi to the North London suburb of Muswell Hill, about eight miles from the centre of London and close to Alexandra Palace, a Victorian edifice of breathtaking vulgarity and the site of the world's first television broadcasts, which now housed an ice-skating rink, an exhibition hall and a floral wine bar which overlooked the local sewage farm.

Why Muswell Hill? Because that was where the now sadly deceased London correspondent had lived, in a company-leased apartment - or flat, as the English call them - in an Edwardian mansion block just off the main thoroughfare, namely Muswell Hill Broadway.

This was not my first time in London. As a young man I had spent two years working as a bookings clerk at the French tourist office in Piccadilly in order to improve my English. At the same time, with the encouragement of my employers, I had toured England, Wales and Scotland, slept in dismal bed-and-*petit-déjeuner* boarding houses from Blackpool to Bournemouth, sampled the local *cuisine* and took a daily constitutional on the rain-swept promenades of many leading British tourist paradises, in order to be able to say (hand on heart) to anyone seeking advice as to the best holiday destinations, that there was really only one choice: *Notre Belle France.*

৵৸

When he heard my accent, the taxi-driver, with the legendary friendliness for which all London taxi-drivers are renowned, punched up the basic fare on his meter and said:

'You're French, right? I've got nothing against you lot - even if you did do the dirty on us in nineteen forty and surrendered to the Krauts. Mind you - fair's fair - that General de Gaulle of yours did try to even things up a bit by forming the Free French Army and having a go himself. But that's all over and done with, right? I mean, what with the European Union and that, we're all united, right? Brothers. No matter what our race, colour or creed. But I have to tell you that I'm a bit pissed off with you Froggies for helping all these so-called asylum seekers to smuggle themselves into Our Sceptred Isle - as the venerable bard Will Whatsit once put it - on account of us being a soft touch compared to you lot.'

I had to admire his honest directness, especially as it

6

turned out that he'd arrived in England from Romania via Hungary, Italy, Belgium and Holland just a few short years ago and had become a British citizen after being put ashore in a rubber dinghy at St Mary's Bay in Kent, in the early hours of the morning. Even to my untutored ears, he seemed to speak in a heavily accented Romanian-Cockney-English *patois* and during the ninety-minute journey from Waterloo to Muswell Hill, via Trafalgar Square, Westminster Bridge, Tower Bridge, Victoria, Hyde Park and Edgware (it appeared that there were substantial roadworks in progress throughout London which prevented him taking a more direct route), the taxi-driver - Constantin by name - philosophised about life, living and the world in general, as all London taxi-drivers or cabbies, as they are called, are prone to do:

'The fing is,' he said: 'The fing *is*, this country is falling apart. And d'you know why? I'll tell you why - because of dishonesty and corruption from top to bottom. The politicians, the money men, the police, even your average man in the street. They're all at it - fiddling their income tax, making false claims on social security, up to their ears in the black economy and flogging gear that's fallen off the back of a lorry.' He paused in full flow: 'That reminds me.' He opened the glove compartment, reached inside, drew out a small cardboard box and handed it to me over his shoulder, through the sliding window.

'Need a new shaver? Brand new. Original box. You can have it for twelve nicker - no, you've been a good pick-up - let's say ten. Robbing meself, mind, but I need the cash. Meeting a geezer in my local rub-a-dub-dub in half an hour who says he'll flog me a few more.'

By now we had finally reached Muswell Hill and as the cab came to a halt outside the apartment block, I paid Constantin what seemed to me to be a great deal of money and said so.

'Yeh, well that's all down to your actual Chancellor of the Exchequer, innit? It's him who raised the fuel prices to pay for his and the Prime Minister's fine wines, fancy food, big cars, country houses, first class travel and trips to Tuscany and that. And who picks up the tab? Honest, hard-working punters like me who have to pay an arm and a leg to fill up their cabs - and you, for having to pay through the nose for a quick trip to Muswell Hill. Night.'

He drove off in a cloud of diesel fumes and, clutching my new electric shaver, I picked up my bags, walked through the main doors of the optimistically named *Arcadia Court* and took the ancient elevator to my fourth floor apartment.

As I opened the door and fumbled for the light switch, the smell of decay was overpowering. It swept through the hallway and out in to the corridor as if trying to escape its own putrefaction. *Quelle Horreur!* For one fleeting, but nevertheless heart-stopping moment, I wondered if, in the absence of anyone to pay for their services, the local funeral directors had simply returned my late predecessor to his place of residence while awaiting further instructions. I edged down the hall and peered into what turned out to be the bedroom. Happily, the unmade bed bore only the *empreinte* of its last occupant and a further inspection of the apartment failed to reveal the half-expected open casket on the dining room table - complete with the mortal remains of my unfortunate colleague - an old English tradition, I am told, to enable the deceased's nearest and dearest to pay their last respects. Face to face, as it were.

Greatly relieved, I sniffed my way further down the hallway, discovering a second bedroom with a sagging double bed, a smaller, but habitable guest bedroom and a kitchen. As I pushed open the kitchen door, I found that the *affreuse odeur* was emanating from an open refrigerator, packed from top to bottom with a wide variety of food and other delicacies, all in an advanced state of decomposition. Why the late Monsieur Didier had failed to close the refrigerator door before leaving the flat for what turned out to be the very last time, I will never know, although an empty *Armagnac* bottle on the kitchen table suggested that prior to his departure, in order to be able to carry out his onerous duties of having to consume large quantities of food and wine for the edification of *Le Courrier's* readers, he may have decided to fortify himself with alcohol.

Whatever the reason, I realised that if I was going to spend the night there, I had to clean up the place as well as I could. But even after emptying the food from the refrigerator into a number of plastic carrier bags, I still had to dispose of them. Where, I wondered, were *les poubelles*, or what the English call dustbins? And then I remembered seeing a row of garbage cans in the small *Residents Only* car park to one side of the main doorway and picking up the packed carrier bags, I entered the elevator and pressed the button for the ground floor. The smell from the bags was already beginning to permeate the elevator interior when, to my dismay, it stopped at the third floor and the door slid open to admit an elderly English couple who nodded politely and re-pressed the button for the ground floor. It took all of three seconds for their noses to twitch in unison, before edging away as far as possible from the source of the *mauvaise odeur* - myself, whom they obviously believed had a serious personal hygiene problem. I forced a smile, indicated the carrier bags and said:

'I do regret the smell, but I have just moved into the block and - '

At the sound of my accent, the couple exchanged a look and the man said:

'You're not English, are you?'

'Well no. I am French actually. And the fact is - '

'French eh?' The couple again looked at each other and nodded sagely, as if my Gallic origins explained everything.

'Yes, well,' said the man: 'Happy New Year anyway.'

The elevator stopped at the ground floor and the door slid open. The elderly couple moved out of the lift with a speed and agility that belied their years and disappeared through the main doors.

My first meeting with fellow residents had hardly got off to an auspicious start and during the following weeks, even though, with typical British old world courtesy, the same couple still continued to nod politely in my direction, if they saw me approaching the elevator, they would invariably scramble for the stairs.

It took me several hours to make the apartment habitable and by then, the old year was almost over and the last thing I wished to do was join the crowds in Muswell Hill Broadway and see in the New Year in a public house or restaurant. As luck would have it, while travelling on the *Eurostar* to London, I'd had the good fortune to get into conversation with an Englishman who lived in the nearby suburb of Crouch End. According to him, Muswell Hill had changed a great deal over the last few years. From being a quiet middle-class backwater, it had become the *au pair* centre of North London and each weekend, young women (of every nationality) strolled along the Broadway in search of a little entertainment. The local young men, also in search of a little entertainment, suddenly realised that Muswell Hill Broadway could well be the answer to their (mostly prurient) pursuits and appeared in their hundreds, packing the relatively new profusion of wine bars, pizza palaces and night clubs, complete with the obligatory bouncers, that now dotted the Broadway. And tonight was New Year's Eve, when everyone would party. It seemed that in the past, the English had always been more concerned with celebrating Christmas rather than the birth of each new year, unlike their Scottish cousins who had always scorned Christmas for what they called 'Hogmanay.' Why they call it that is, I was told, lost in the mists of time, but accordingly, the Scots had long declared New Year's Day to be a public holiday, presumably to enable those North of the border to sleep off the alcoholic indulgences of the previous evening.

But after the English Parliament had also declared New Year's Day to be a public holiday, it appeared that the once relatively temperate English had eagerly embraced the opportunity of getting as *saoul* - or as rat-arsed, as my Crouch End acquaintance quaintly described it - as even the most dedicated of Scottish imbibers. And from the shouting, raucous singing, police sirens and sounds of breaking bottles coming from the direction of the Broadway, his description seemed to be rather apt.

Thus I decided to make an early night of it and retired to the guest room. Midnight came and went and I was just on the point of slipping into the arms of Morpheus, when there was a loud banging on my front door. I slipped on my *robe de chambre* and went to the door. Through the convex glass spy-

11

hole, I saw the somewhat distorted face of a youngish man wearing a paper hat with tinsel stars and an expression of cheerful *bonhomie*.

'Who is it?' I called.

'It's only me, Mr Didier. Malcolm from number forty-two. Mother sent me to be your first footer.'

First footer? What on earth was that? But as he had obviously been acquainted with the late Antoine Didier and looked fairly harmless, I opened the door. He was, I suppose, in his middle thirties. A small, rather skinny man with a shock of gingery hair and a pair of steel-rimmed spectacles. He was wearing what I later found out to be a hand-knitted paisley pullover, an old tweed sports jacket and a food-stained necktie. He beamed cheerfully and held out his hand. As I shook it, he said:

'Happy New Year, Mr Didier.' Then he paused, pushed his face close to mine, squinted through his spectacles and said, accusingly: 'You're not Mr Didier.'

'I know. I'm Pierre LaPoste. Antoine's replacement.'

'Oh. I see. Been called back to Head Office, has he?'

'In a manner of speaking, yes.'

'So you must be French, too.'

'Yes.'

He smiled, winked, then in schoolboy French and with an atrocious accent, he said: *'Où est la plume de ma tante* and all that, eh?'

I later learned that when taking first-year French, generations of British school children had been urged to show concern about the whereabouts of the pen of their aunt, whether or not they had an aunt or if she'd even mislaid her pen.

He continued: 'Mother will be sad. She found your

colleague to be most charming. And I must say, she'll be very disappointed that he didn't even drop in to say goodbye.'

'I don't think he had much choice, Mr... er... Malcolm, is it?'

'Malcolm Nesbitt. My mother's Mrs. Nesbitt,' he added unnecessarily.

'The fact is,' I continued carefully, anxious to cushion the shock of what I had to tell him: 'Antoine has gone to a better place.'

'So you said.'

'No, I mean he's departed this mortal coil.' He looked at me uncomprehendingly: 'He has passed on.' Still no reaction. How could anyone be that obtuse? *'Il est Mort!'* I continued, with rising desperation. Then suddenly remembering an overheard English euphemism for the final journey: 'He's snuffed it!'

His brow cleared: 'Oh, so he's dead. No wonder I hadn't seen him around for the past two or three weeks.' He put his hand in his pocket and drew out what looked to be a piece of coal: 'You'd better have this then.'

'What is it?'

'It's a piece of coal - at least it should have been a piece of coal, but we've got central heating you see, so mother told me to find a bit of rock and paint it black and that's what I did.' Slightly baffled, I thanked him, but as I took the proffered piece of rock, he added warningly: 'Careful how you hold it - the paint's still a bit wet - but it's the thought that counts, isn't it?'

By now I was more than slightly baffled: 'Well, this is very kind of you, but I'm afraid I don't understand the significance of this piece of coal - or rather, this rock covered with sticky black paint.'

He looked at me in surprise, then he smiled and nodded sympathetically: 'Of course, you're French, aren't you? Well, it's an old Scottish tradition. The first person to cross your threshold on New Year's Day is what we call a first footer. Someone to wish you a Happy New Year and all the luck in the world.'

'Ah. So you're Scottish.'

'I should think not!' He gave a sudden bray of laughter, obviously finding the mere idea to be extremely amusing: 'I'm English. Born and bred in Muswell Hill. Like my mother. Genuine Muswell Hillbillies, as you might say. We just think it's a nice way of ushering in the New Year.'

'But what's the piece of coal for?'

He thought for a moment, then said: 'That's a point. To be honest, I haven't got a clue.'

'So what am I supposed to do with it?'

'Whatever you would like to do with it.'

By now I already knew what I'd like to do with it, but the man was, after all, a neighbour and his appearance at my front door had obviously been prompted by the best of motives.

'Look, my friend,' I said: 'I'd invite you in for a drink, but I only arrived here last night and there's not a drop in the flat.'

'That's all right,' said Malcolm: 'I don't drink. Apart from cocoa. Cranberry juice. And water, of course. Oh yes. Plenty of water.' He nodded his head enthusiastically: 'What would we do without water, eh?'

The conversation was getting more absurd by the minute.

'Yes well,' I said: 'Thank you for being my first footer and please thank your mother for thinking of me.'

'Oh she wasn't thinking of you. She was thinking of Mr Didier. And she would have come herself if her legs hadn't started weeping again. And that, of course, means lots of fresh bandages. She's a martyr to those legs of hers, is mother.'

I tried to dispel the sudden image of a presumably overweight old lady desperately trying to stem the flow of fluid from her lower limbs - and failed.

'Yes, well,' I said again: 'Wish her a very happy New Year from me and perhaps we'll meet up in the near future.'

He nodded brightly and turned away. As he did so, he obviously remembered something and turned back.

'Oh yes,' he said: 'Tea. And coffee. Decaffeinated, of course. And the occasional cup of hot milk. '

'What about them?'

'I drink those, too.'

'Ah,' I said, and for want of a better response: 'Good.'

He gave another nod, another smile and a final 'goodnight.'

After I'd managed to wash most of the black paint from my fingers, I went back to bed. But it was another couple of hours before I managed to drop off to sleep, the image of those weeping legs still refusing to fade away. I began to wonder if my other neighbours would turn out to be as... unusual as the Nesbitts. They did.

The following morning, I woke up refreshed, but hungry. As the only food in the immediate vicinity now resided at the bottom of a garbage can, I set out to find a suitable *café* for my *petit déjeuner*. I was unsuccessful. The only establishment open on New Year's Day at that time of the morning was the aforementioned Sid's Diner, a small, neon-lit, red-plastic-tabled establishment halfway along the Broadway. Even though it did lack that vital ambience which made dining an event rather than a necessity, I pushed open the door and went in.

The only other customer was an elderly man in a grubby raincoat, wheezing over an empty plate and a cup of tea as he stubbed out a series of cigarettes into an over-flowing ashtray. I sat down at a table as far away from the chain-smoker as possible, picked up the bill of fare, attempted to decipher what was on offer - and failed - defeated by the wide variety of soup and coffee stains, bits of dried food and grimy fingerprints which decorated the *menu* from top to bottom.

I looked around for assistance and tried to catch the eye of the small, fat man in a chef's off-white jacket, sitting behind the glass counter, his face buried in a newspaper, whom I assumed to be Sid himself. I coughed politely. There was no response. I coughed again and without raising his eyes from his newspaper, Sid said:

'I'd cut down, if I were you, Harry.'

The elderly man in the raincoat lit another cigarette and said:

'That weren't me. It was him.'

'Him who?'

Sid finally raised his eyes from his newspaper and peered in my direction:

'Oh. Sorry, mate. Didn't see you come in. What are you after - the Special?'

'What is that?'

'Two eggs, bacon, fried bread, sausage, beans, cuppa tea or coffee - two forty-nine.'

'Ah,' I said, with an inward wince: 'No thank you. I'm not that hungry. I'll just have a couple of *croissants* and a *café noire.*'

'Not in here, you won't, mate. Where you from?'

'France.'

'Yeh well, this is Sid's Diner, not the Eiffel-bleedin' Tower. We serve proper traditional English nosh in this place - not poncey French muck like - what was that again?'

'*Croissants*. And filter coffee.'

'Well whatever. So d'you want it or not?'

'What?'

'The Special.'

I hesitated. It had been a long time since my last meal and as *Sid's Diner* seemed to be the only establishment open in the immediate vicinity, there seemed to be little choice.

I said: 'What else is there?'

Sid considered: 'Well, if you don't fancy the Special, there's egg and chips, steak and chips, chop and chips, bacon and chips, sausage and chips and fish-and-chips. Or you could always have the mixed grill.'

I sighed. I had an idea what was coming: 'What's that then, Mr Sid? - no, don't tell me - egg, steak, chop, bacon, sausage, fish-and-chips - *oui*?'

'Wee. And it's Charlie.'

'What?'

'The name's Charlie. Sid passed away a couple of years back.'

From what? I wondered. Acute cholesterolitis?

'Yeh. I bought the place off-of his widow but I kept the name. I mean, you can't put a price on goodwill, can you?' He got to his feet: 'So what's it to be?'

'The Special.'

As I said, in the circumstances, I really had no choice.

In the cold light of day, I was now able to inspect the

company flat in greater detail and it was, I regret to say, in very poor condition. The late Antoine Didier seemed to have cared little for his immediate surroundings and the *décoration* was execrable, with peeling wallpaper in the main living room and chipped paintwork that had not come into contact with a paintbrush for many years. The ceiling was tobacco coloured, which was not surprising, considering the numerous cigarette burns on most of the chairs, tables and furniture. Didier had obviously been as dedicated a smoker as he was a *bon viveur* and the colour of the ceiling was a memorial to both himself and *Gauloise Papier Maïs*.

For a moment I thought wistfully of my little house in Ménerbes with its comfortable, chintz-covered furniture, its Persian rugs on cool stone floors and my carefully chosen collection of paintings of the Lubéron by local artists. There and then I decided to inform Head Office that I was not prepared to live in a property that had been allowed to deteriorate to the level of a seedy back street hovel in *Vieux Marseilles* and that they either allowed me to move into a more salubrious apartment, or give me the authority to engage the services of local painters, decorators and any other artisans I needed to renovate the flat to an acceptable standard.

The reply from Head Office was not long in coming. *Les comptables* - the accountants - had done their sums and it appeared that the long lease on the apartment was now ridiculously cheap compared to other, similar properties in the area and, to maintain the value of their investment, they grudgingly agreed to allow me to employ local craftsmen to do what was necessary to bring the apartment up to a liveable standard and replace the worn-out furniture, carpets and drapes. With the usual accountants' thoroughness bordering on zealotry, it transpired that they had also checked out British furniture prices via the Internet and I was instructed to eschew such illustrious establishments as *Heals, Habitat* and *Harrods* and visit a company called *Reg's Repossessions*, which apparently specialised in second hand furniture and was based in Finsbury Park, a short bus journey away from Muswell Hill.

But that was to be some time in the future. My first task was to find suitable craftsmen who would restore the apartment to what it once was. But when, where and how did one find local craftsmen who possessed the professional expertise I so urgently required? The answer soon became patently obvious: with great difficulty. A glance through a fading copy of the *North London Yellow Pages* (circa 1982) which was propping up one corner of the dining room table, revealed a plethora of entries and advertisements for local tradesmen, all claiming to be master craftsmen who would take care of my needs quickly, efficiently and at a very competitive price. I pulled the telephone towards me and began to dial.

I soon discovered that London telephone numbers had been changed at least twice over the last couple of decades and it took some time before I was able to make my first connection, only to find that the premises of *Rumbold & Fishwick, Painters and Decorators*, in the nearby Archway Road, were now occupied by *The Good Earth Oriental Restaurant*, where one could presumably eat dirt cheap, so to speak. It took many more telephone calls and a great deal of patience before I finally made contact with a builder, painter and decorator who claimed that I'd telephoned him at just the right moment, having just completed his last job that very same morning. True to his word, he arrived on the doorstep on the dot of two pm, his notebook at the ready to take down the information needed to submit an estimate for the work and materials involved. I found this to be extremely encouraging, because as the English writer in Ménerbes had quickly discovered, the local craftsmen of the Lubéron were not noted for their reliability. But in England, things were obviously very different.

At first sight, Alfred Moscrop did not appear to be a happy man. A short, thick-set, balding man in his middle forties with a permanent expression of total resignation, he walked through the front door, sniffed the air, shook his head sadly and said:

'How long have you had dry rot?'

'I didn't know I had dry rot.'

'You've got it all right, squire. The whole building's got it. Riddled with it. From top to bottom.'

I sniffed the air: 'I can't smell anything.'

'You will.' He licked the stub of his pencil: 'Now what are you after?'

I told him. He peered morosely at the peeling wallpaper, scribbled a few notes and said: 'You know it's live?'

'What is?'

'The plaster. Strip off the wallpaper and the whole lot will come down.' He switched his gaze to the nearest radiator: 'And another thing. Who put that central heating in?'

'No idea.'

'Well I'll tell you - whoever it was, he wants locking up.'

'But can you fix it?'

'Oh, I can fix it all right - but it'll cost you.'

His estimate arrived the following day and by the end of the week, a fax from Head Office gave me the go-ahead. It seemed that compared to French prices, the cost was not exorbitant. I picked up the telephone.

'Right then, Mr Moscrop,' I said: 'When can you start?'

'Tomorrow,' he said: 'Eight o-clock sharp.'

Impressed by his typically English, quietly-spoken professionalism, I set the alarm for seven-thirty. French tradesmen obviously had a lot to learn from their contemporaries *Anglais*.

FEBRUARY

IT RAINED IN FEBRUARY. It had also rained in January. From New Year's Day onwards and as January became February, I was still sitting amid the original squalor of the living room, waiting for the Quietly-Spoken English Professional to show up. Attempts to contact him over the last few weeks had been thwarted by a mobile telephone that was permanently switched off, a telephone answering machine that never answered messages and a fax machine that appeared to be perpetually engaged.

Mr Alfred Moscrop, of *Moscrop & Son, Master Builders, Painters and Decorators* (as the *Yellow Pages* entry had claimed) had seemingly disappeared off the face of the planet. Why, I wondered, had he taken the time and trouble to inspect the apartment, prepare an estimate and give a start-date for the work involved, when it now seemed that he'd had no intention of turning up? Could it be that (like many of his French counterparts, it has to be said), he was a covert sadist who, in the American vernacular, got his rocks off by raising clients' hopes then letting them down with a sickening thud?

I offered a silent apology to those much maligned craftsmen of the Lubéron, walked over to the window and gazed out over the rain-swept rooftops of Muswell Hill. It was not a pleasant day. The sullen dark clouds that had gathered over Alexandra Palace were tinkling steadily on to the parkland below and, not for the first time, I felt an almost physical twinge of home-sickness. It wasn't so much the rain or the absence of blue skies, it was the *type* of rain - a thin, mean, non-stop drizzle from a celestial watering-can that soaked everything but washed away nothing - unlike the Lubéron's short but intense downpours during the *Mistral*.

Although tied to the apartment in case *Moscrop et Fils* finally decided to turn up, I was still very conscious of the fact that I was in England to do a job and I thus secured the approval of *Le Courrier's* travel editor to write a series of articles on English traditional dishes, lifting most of the basic information from the interminable British television programmes about cooks and cooking and plagiarising a wide variety of British cookery books - both ancient and modern - from the local library.

I had got the idea after a second visit by Malcolm Nesbitt, my neighbour from number forty-two, who had come to ask me if I would care to accompany him on one of his fungi hunting missions in nearby Alexandra Park. I was quite surprised. In Provence, the wild fungi season was in late March.

'Wild truffles?' I said doubtfully: 'In February?'

Malcolm gave his usual braying laugh:

'Oh dearie me no. Not truffles. Mushrooms. Or *champignons* as I believe you people call them. But you're quite right. The wild fungi season over here is more autumnal and should have been over weeks ago. But it's been such a mild winter, you never know your luck. We'll use Alice.'

'Alice?'

'To sniff them out. Like you use pigs to snuff out truffles, right?'

'Well, usually, yes.'

'But as mother and I don't keep pigs - oh dear me, no - ' He brayed again at the very idea: 'Where would we put them? No, we use Alice. She's the one who does the sniffing for us. She'll sniff out anything, will Alice.'

Before I could ascertain if Alice was a relative, close friend or neighbour, he explained that she happened to be a small dog of unknown parentage with an undoubted skill at sniffing everything within walking distance of the little-known corner of Alexandra Park, where, when walking Alice a couple of years ago, she had sniffed out a cache of wild mushrooms in the long grass. It appeared that the area had once been part of the now defunct Alexandra Palace race course, upon which generations of horses had deposited enough *fumier* to gladden the heart of any ardent *amateur de champignons*, past, present and future.

As Malcolm's expedition could, I reasoned, provide a nice little piece for *Le Courrier* in a thin week, I agreed to accompany him and with the small, rather scruffy Alice snapping at my ankles, off we went. After sniffing a wide variety of trees, lamposts, the *derrières* of several quadruped acquaintances and countless deposits of *déjections canines*, Alice finally led us to Malcolm's secret corner where, to my surprise, she immediately uncovered a small ring of edible wild *psalliota campestris*, buried deep within the long grass. It obviously *had* been an unusually mild winter. Unfortunately however, before we'd had time to harvest them, Alice urinated delicately over each and every one of them. Malcolm just chuckled and said:

'Not to worry. It'll soon wash off.'

Which will explain, I trust, on being invited to join Malcolm and his mother to partake of traditional English pancakes on the following Shrove Tuesday, why I was at pains to discover if recently-gathered wild mushrooms were part of the traditional English pancake recipe. As it seemed they weren't, I extracted a bottle from the late Antoine Didier's stock of *Cabernet Sauvignon* and rang the doorbell of number forty-two.

I had earlier established that Shrove Tuesday was a peculiarly English feast day when it was customary for people to be shriven - or prevailed upon to make their confessions - in preparation for Lent. And having been duly shriven, custom had it that they then unshrivelled themselves by consuming large quantities of lemon pancakes, which again presented the possible basis for an amusing little piece for *Le Courrier*.

As I had surmised, the long-widowed Mrs Nesbitt turned out to be a very large, very overweight woman with wispy hair and watery grey eyes who sat - or rather held court - in a large armchair, her weeping legs mercifully obscured by a thick blanket. In her lap squatted the beady-eyed Alice who stared at me unblinkingly throughout the entire evening, obviously still brooding about the discreet backward kicks I'd been obliged to give her behind Malcolm's back during the fungi expedition, to discourage her from savaging my ankles. The *décoration* of the Nesbitts' apartment was pure 1930s, with dark brown paintwork, parquet flooring and a three-piece suite in uncut moquette. At Malcolm's introduction, Mrs Nesbitt gave me a brief nod, looked me up and down and said, pointedly:

'I liked Mr Didier.'

The implication was obvious. Monsieur Didier one. Pierre LaPoste nil.

Malcolm Nesbitt suddenly appeared from the adjoining kitchen holding a large frying pan in which bubbled a huge yellow pancake and said:

'This is the tricky bit. I have to toss it.'

'How d'you mean, toss it?'

'Turn it over in mid-air and catch it again. It's all part of the ancient custom.'

'Why can't you simply turn it over with a spatula?'

His mother sniffed: 'And spoil all the enjoyment? Really, Mr LaPoste, have the French no sense of tradition?' She nodded towards her son: 'Off you go, Malcolm.'

Malcolm took a deep breath, weighed the frying pan in his hands and suddenly tossed the pancake into the air. For a moment, it hovered under the central lampshade, then without turning over, it fell like a greasy yellow blanket towards the floor, neatly evading Malcolm's waiting frying pan and finally draping itself over one of the uncut moquette armchairs. Malcolm appeared to regard this as all part of the fun and, not for the first time, he chuckled and said:

'Not to worry. It'll soon wash off.'

In the ordinary way I would, in the *patois* of *journalese internationale*, have immediately made my excuses and left, but the Nesbitts were, after all, my neighbours and they'd obviously meant well by inviting me to a traditional English pancake party. In fact, once the bits of fluff from the uncut moquette had been removed, the pancake, soaked in sugar and lemon juice was quite delicious and when I complimented the chef, a surprised Malcolm said:

'But surely, you have them in France?'

'Of course.'

'What are French pancakes like?' demanded Mrs Nesbitt.

'*Crèpes.*'

'Oh come now,' said Malcolm: 'They can't be that bad.'

'*Crèpes,*' I enunciated carefully: 'That's what our pancakes are called. *Crèpes.* As in *Crèpes Suzettes.*'

'Ah,' said Malcolm: 'Got you.'

It was not an unpleasant evening. Mrs Nesbitt finally seemed to warm to me if only because I made a point of kissing her hand, Gallic fashion, before departing.

'Oh la-la,' she said, with a girlish little giggle: 'That's what Mr Didier used to do.'

It appeared that Mrs. Nesbitt was locked in a Charles Boyer time-warp and a Frenchman who didn't kiss hands was, to her mind, unworthy of his nationality. Almost, I thought, as Alfred Moscop, *Master Builder, Painter and Decorator,* was as unworthy of his.

✿

By now, I'd had enough of the elusive Mr Moscrop, but the following morning, just as I reached for the *Yellow Pages* in an attempt to find a replacement, the doorbell rang. As he walked through the door, holding one end of a wooden ladder, the elusive Mr Moscrop called over his shoulder to his unseen helper:

'All right, Tarquin, down your end. I'll take it from here.'

'Down my end, Dad,' said a disembodied voice from the hallway and the ladder was lowered to the floor.

Said Moscrop: 'You go back to the van and start bringing up the rest of the stuff.'

'The rest of the stuff. Yes. Right. You got it, Dad,' said

the voice obligingly.

Moscrop sighed and addressed the open door: 'No, Tarquin. I haven't got it. But I will have, once you bring it up.'

'I know that Dad. When I said I'd got it, I didn't mean I'd got it. I meant -

Moscrop sighed again: 'Just get on with it, will you? We don't want to fall behind schedule, do we?'

'Yes. Right.'

I stared at Moscrop in disbelief:

'But you already are behind schedule, Mr Moscrop. By about three weeks.'

There was the patter of squeaky trainers running down the stairs. Moscrop dragged the rest of the ladder into the hall, looked pointedly at his watch and said:

'Only technically.'

'What d'you mean, only technically?'

He looked at me pityingly and, as if explaining the theory of relativity to a retarded *grenouille*, he said patiently:

'I may not have been here in person *per se*, but I've been very much on the job. It's called preparation. Securing the right materials, the right equipment, the right... er, the right thingies and that. You can't rush these things. Not if you want a proper job.' He looked around him: 'I think we should make a start on the kitchen. Get rid of the fungus under the sink.'

'I didn't know there was any fungus under the sink.'

'There will be, squire. You take my word for it.'

I followed him into the kitchen. He went straight over to the sink, picked up the electric kettle, filled it with water, switched it on and looked towards the cupboards, enquiringly:

'Where d'you keep it?'

'Keep what?'

He looked at me in surprise: 'The tea. And coffee. Show me where it is and I won't have to bother you again.'

His impertinence was breathtaking: 'Now look here,' I said.

He held up his hand: 'Course, being French you wouldn't know about that, would you?'

'About what?'

'Our English traditions in the workplace. Regular cups of tea and coffee for us horny-handed sons of toil is what oils the wheels of British industry. Goes all the way back to the Industrial Revolution. It's what is called *C&P* - Custom and Practice. Now where is it?'

While I was sure he was talking a lot of *merde*, I had no wish to alienate him on his very first day. Any horny-handed son of toil is better than none at all. Cravenly, I pointed towards the corner cupboard:

'In there.'

Well, when in Muswell Hill...

When I was eventually able to put a face to the disembodied voice of Moscrop junior, he turned out to a cheerfully feckless 23-year-old with a bare midriff, torn jeans, a too-short tee-shirt and an inane grin. The current fashion amongst British building workers is, it seems, to dress in such a way as to ensure that a pronounced upper-buttock cleavage is always clearly visible, whatever the weather.

To complete his ensemble, Tarquin Moscrop affected spiky hair, a tattoo of a hooded cobra encircling his right forearm, a silver stud through his left nostril and a gold ring through what the English amusingly call 'the belly button.'

Moscrop senior caught my open-mouthed gaze towards his colourful offspring and said, defensively: 'He's not a bad lad, you know.'

If only to avoid the possibility of his son's appearance frightening off his more sensitive clients, he obviously felt it incumbent upon him to explain that it was nothing more than the need of a young man to "do his own thing." But by the way he occasionally looked at him, with an expression of despair and resignation, I got the distinct impression that Moscrop senior was not too enamoured of his son's fashion statement.

Yet, whatever his outward appearance, the boy was a willing enough worker and attacked his tasks with an enthusiasm bordering on the manic and once *Moscrop et Fils* had started work, it soon became abundantly clear that I would have to move out until after they'd finished.

By the end of the first day, a thin layer of plaster dust had crept into every niche and corner of the apartment and while Moscrop senior supervised from a safe distance, his son bravely hacked at the walls, covering himself from head to foot in the ash-like powder. Within minutes, red-rimmed of eye and ashen of face, Moscrop junior had assumed the appearance of a leading member of the walking dead in an old black-and-white horror movie and, when he ventured out into the hallway to bring in another piece of equipment, a piercing shriek from a passing female neighbour proved that I wasn't alone in thinking so.

It was obvious that I couldn't possibly eat, sleep and write in an apartment that now resembled a lunar landscape and I resolved to find temporary accommodation. But where? When I explained my problem to Monsieur Moscrop, he nodded sympathetically and said:

'A bed-sitter do you?'

'Well yes. I suppose so.'

'Mrs Kwiatkowska.'

'Pardon?'

'Polish lady. Runs a private guest house. Just three minutes away. We did her drains last April. She'll fix you up.'

'Even though I'll only be needing it for a short time?'

He grinned: 'Half an hour short enough for you?'

'I do not understand.'

'At the *Savoy* guest house, you can rent a room by the hour. And a lot of people do. When me and Tarquin were doing the drains, they was coming and going all day long. Very popular place, The *Savoy*.'

'What sort of people?'

'Businessmen. Their secretaries. There for conferences, interviews, things like that. Then you've got your local housewives, who turn up with their personal masseurs and fitness trainers - for one-to-one workouts in private, I suppose. Should suit you down to the ground. Tell Mrs Kwiatkowska I sent you and you'll be all right.'

I hesitated. Though there are many such establishments in France - in Paris in particular - which happily cater for both long-term residents and those whose requirements are of a more fleeting nature, I was surprised by Moscrop senior's *naiveté* in not seeing this guest house for what it obviously was. But with his son within earshot, it did not seem proper to point out that the comings and goings of so many local residents would appear to indicate that a great deal more than shorthand typing, personal massage and press-ups took place behind the closed doors of The *Savoy Private Guest House*.

But at least it was close by, which would enable me to constantly check on the Moscrops' progress. And it would, presumably, work out a little cheaper than a room in one of the small local hotels. At *Le Courrier de Paris*, as everywhere else throughout Europe, *le comptable* ruled.

'Very well,' I said: 'I'll give it a try.'

Moscrop glanced towards his son, gave me a wink, followed by a metaphorical nudge in the ribs, lowered his voice and said:

'Thought you might, squire.'

༺༄༺

The *Savoy Private Guest House* was situated in one of the five roads that radiate from the bus-terminus roundabout in the very centre of Muswell Hill and, as Alfred Moscrop had said, was just minutes away from the apartment. From the outside, The *Savoy* bore little resemblance to its more illustrious namesake in the heart of London, being a towering Victorian edifice on five floors plus a *grenier* - an attic - and a converted basement which had probably once served as a coal cellar.

A partially-illuminated glass sign hung drunkenly from a support over the front door, announcing that there were *VA..NCI.S*, which I took to mean vacancies. As I climbed the short flight of steps to the front entrance, my hastily-packed suitcase in one hand and my laptop computer in the other, I began to wonder just what I was letting myself in for. Again, I hesitated, but reminding myself that needs must when the accountant drives, I rang the doorbell. Even though I could hear the bell ringing somewhere deep inside the guest house, there was no reply. I rang again. Still no reply and with a feeling of some relief I turned away, intent on finding somewhere a little more salubrious.

The voice was loud, impatient and seemed to come from out of nowhere.

'Yes?'

I looked around me. I saw no one. The voice called again:

'Down here.'

I looked over the doorstep balustrade to see a woman of indeterminate age standing outside the basement door and glaring up at me. She wore a grubby housecoat and was puffing on a cigarette in a long bamboo cigarette holder. Her accent was strong and presumably Polish.

'What you want?'

'Madame Kwiatkowska? Monsieur Moscrop - the builder - said you might have a room for me.'

She tapped the ash from her cigarette into her housecoat pocket, turned briefly towards the open door and bellowed:

'Ernie? Ernie!'

A moment later, a middle-aged, white-faced little man, wearing baggy trousers and braces over a collarless shirt, emerged through the door and said irritably:

'Now what?'

'Show him the first floor back.'

With that, she brushed past him back into the house and as he wearily climbed the stone steps up to the street, he complained bitterly to the world at large:

'Do this, do that. Sweep the stairs, unblock the karzy...' He addressed the basement door: 'God love-us, Gloria, I've only got two pairs of hands, you know.' He reached the pavement and trudged up the steps towards me, repeating plaintively: 'I've only got two pairs of hands, you know.'

I assumed mathematics were not Monsieur Ernie's strong-point and showed as much sympathy as I could in the circumstances:

'Hmm yes,' I said. And for want of something better to say: 'Must be quite a handicap.'

He fumbled for the front door key from a large, clanking, metal key ring and said:

'You foreign?'

'French.'

He nodded towards the basement:

'She's foreign, too. Her down below. Polish. Course, Gloria's not her real name.'

'Oh?' I said politely: 'What is it, then?'

'Dunno,' he said: 'Never been able to pronounce it.'

The conversation was becoming as bizarre as the one I had with my first-footing neighbour on New Year's Eve, but I still couldn't help asking:

'You really can't pronounce your wife's first name?'

'Wife?' he repeated: 'Wife? Do me a favour, matey. She's just my fancy woman.'

He opened the door, jerked his head and I walked past him into the front hall. He followed, muttering darkly under his breath, obviously deeply aggrieved that I could even think he was married to the formidable Mrs Kwiatkowska.

The room was surprisingly clean and comfortably furnished, with an *en suite* shower and tiny kitchenette. It seemed ideal for my temporary needs. Unfortunately, however, when Ernie informed me of the weekly rental, I knew immediately that it was a little more than *Le Courrier's* accountants would be prepared to pay. Sadly, I was about to pick up my luggage and depart, when there was a loud rapping on the room door. Before either of us could answer it, it was abruptly pushed open by two extremely pretty, extremely shapely young women, both identically dressed in nurses' uniforms and who, in addition, happened to be identical in every other way. As they walked into the room, they gave an airy wave of the hand in my direction and said to Ernie:

'You want to get that lock fixed, Ernie. Anyone could just walk straight in here.' To me, they said: 'Welcome to Muswell Hill's very own den of iniquity. Not much to look at, but a lot of fun. We're the Seymour sisters. We've got the room across the landing.'

'I'm Cindy,' said one.

'And I'm Angie,' said her facsimile.

'They're twins,' volunteered Ernie.

'I think he might have already worked that out for himself,' said Cindy.

But Ernie was determined to be informative and as if by way of explanation for their forthright manner, he continued:

'They're from Manchester. And they're nurses. Real ones, I mean. Not like her who books the second floor front every Friday afternoon to play doctors and nurses.'

Said Cindy: 'We work at the Whittington. The hospital on Highgate Hill. The one that was named after Dick.'

'Dick?'

Angie giggled: 'Dick Whittington, sillee. Him and his cat who became Lord Mayor of London.'

By now, I was totally confused: 'A cat became Lord Mayor of London?'

It was Cindy's turn to giggle: 'You having us on?'

'No. I assure you - '

Angie interposed: 'The thing is, when Mrs K told us that someone new might be moving in today, we thought we'd better look you over.'

'Make sure you were an improvement on the last tenant.' said Cindy.

'Dirty old bugger,' said Angie.

'Used to look through the key-hole when we were taking a shower,' said Cindy.

Said Angie: 'Where are you from, sunshine?'

'France.'

'That's all right, then, isn't it, Ange?' said Cindy: 'I mean, why should he want to cop an eyeful through a key-hole when he's got all those nude beaches and the *Folies Bergères* back home?'

'Why indeed?' I said, reassuringly, even though by now, I had every sympathy with the previous tenant's desire to cop an eyeful, as Cindy had so quaintly put it. Undoubtedly, the nubile Seymour sisters were clearly the stuff from which superior sexual fantasies were made and whatever prurient feelings I still had for the plumply-pretty Michelle from the Ménerbes *pâtisserie*, they suddenly evaporated in the heady scent from the twins' shower gel. I turned to Ernie, took out my wallet and said:

'I'll take it.'

After all, I reasoned, any journalist worth his *sel* should be able to fiddle his expenses to make up the difference. So to *le diable* with the *Le Courrier's* accountants. Just who did they think they were?

❧❧

That evening, seated at my computer, I was well into the piece about the somewhat eccentric English ritual of Shrove Tuesday pancake-tossing, which I would then send to *Le*

Courrier by e-mail, when there came a discreet tapping on my door.

For a moment, I wondered if this heralded a social visit from one - or even both - of the Seymour sisters who, after being up to their elbows in bed-pans all day (in a manner of speaking), sought a little light conversation with the new resident. I quickly checked my appearance in the mirror, assumed a roguishly laid-back *homme du monde* posture on the couch and called, huskily:

'*Entrez.*'

Too late, I remembered that if my visitor or visitors were the Seymour sisters, they would not have wasted time knocking on the door, but simply pushed it open and walked in, as they had done previously. Even so, I still couldn't help feeling rather disappointed when the door opened to reveal Madame Kwiatkowska's absurdly-called fancy man. He glanced furtively over his shoulder, slid into the room, closed the door firmly behind him and stood with his back to it.

'Yes, Mr Ernie?' I said politely.

'Just dropped in to see if you're settling in all right and if you needed anything.'

'Well, I'd be most grateful if you would fix the door lock, but apart from that...'

Ernie shook his head: 'I didn't mean that sort of thing. I meant...' his voice dropped an octave: 'Other things.'

'Such as?'

'You know... other things.'

I was about to point out that the conversation did not seem to be getting anywhere, when the *euro* finally dropped. So Monsieur Ernie was not only The *Savoy's* janitor, he was also its part-time procurer, too. While I had never felt strongly - either for or against - the activities of the oldest profession, I believed I was still young enough, presentable enough and with more than enough *virilité* to attract the opposite sex without the need for money to change hands.

'I'm sorry,' I said firmly: 'If you mean what I think you mean, you've got the wrong person.'

He thought for a minute, then said: 'What do you think I mean?'

'Let me just say *merci beaucoup* for your kind offer, but that I have no desire for female company at the moment.'

He looked quite shocked: 'You mean you think I'm a ponce? Well, that's nice, innit? I don't even know anyone of that persuasion.' He seemed genuinely aggrieved at my suggestion: 'I come here to try and do you a favour and you think I'm pimping for her in the second floor front, her in third floor back and them in the second floor double. You're right out of order, matey. What I came for is to ask you if you're short of anything.'

'Like what?'

'Mini hi-fi gear. Radios. Small TVs. Shavers - anything that's portable. Just say the word and they're yours. At a very competitive price.'

'Shavers?' I repeated. I had a suddenly feeling of *déjà-vu*. Perhaps Ernie and the Cockney-Romanian cab driver shared the same supplier.

'You want one?' he asked eagerly.

'I've just bought one.'

He looked so downcast that, still feeling a little guilty over the misunderstanding during which I implied he was a part-time *souteneur* and remembering that the only radio to which I had access was under a dust sheet in the apartment, I said: 'I could use a small radio. One that could get the news from *France Inter*.'

'Say no more. What time d'you go to your scratcher?'

'My scratcher?'

'Bed.'

'Ah. Not till late.'

'I'll be back then.'

He turned to open the door then turned back again.

'Look, um, there's no need to mention this to her down below. Doesn't like me making a few quid on the side - in case I spend it on other women.' He gave a mirthless smile: 'Other women? That's a laugh. I wouldn't have the strength.' And with weary resignation: 'You may not think it by looking at her, but she's very... demanding is Gloria. Like a thing possessed when the mood takes her. Sometimes, I've hardly got a body to call my own.'

He opened the door, peered out into the corridor, then hissed: 'See you later.' The door closed behind him and I went back to my computer.

❧

Two hours later, the article finished and ready for e-mailing, I was about to pour myself a large brandy, when the door burst open and the comely Seymour sisters walked - or rather sashayed - straight in, one bearing a plate of what appeared to be half a ham, pineapple, sausage and anchovy pizza, the other with a portion of what I found out later to be a traditional English dish called Manchester Tart.

Said Cindy: 'Bet you haven't eaten anything all day, have you?'

'Well no,' I admitted: 'I've been too busy.'

Said Angie to her sister: 'Told you so.'

They placed the dishes in front of me.

'Then get that down you. It'll put ink in your ball-point.'

While I was not acquainted with the expression, it wasn't too difficult to work out what she meant and I felt quite touched by their thoughtfulness.

'This is very kind of you,' I began.

'No it isn't,' interrupted Cindy: 'They're only left-overs.'

'And it was either give them to you or flush them down the toilet.'

But it was, as Malcolm Nesbitt had said, the thought that counted and I was beginning to feel rather hungry. As I started to eat, they plumped themselves on the bed and watched me with a joint expression that, sadly, could only be described as one of maternal concern, rather than the hoped-for look of avid hunger for what my masculinity had to offer. It was clear that despite the widely-known fact (in France at least) that all English women invariably go weak at the knees at the sound of a French accent, so far, my Gallic charm had obviously had little or no impact on the delectable *Belles Anglais*. Rather despondently, I finished most of the pizza and pulled the Manchester Tart towards me.

'We're not keeping you up, are we?' said Angie.

'No, no,' I said: 'I've got to wait up for Mr Ernie. He's bringing me something.'

Cindy gave a little gasp of dismay, jumped up from the bed and said:

'Oh God. Did you hear that, Ange? Ernie's bringing him something.'

Said Angie: 'I heard.' To me, she said: 'What's he bringing you then? Shaver? Walkman? Mobile phone?'

'A radio.'

'Well tell him to put it where the sun don't shine. Or you could end up in the nick.'

'The nick?'

'Jail, prison, the *Bastille* - sharing a cell with Ernie. Didn't you know he's an old lag - a professional criminal? He's spent more time inside the pokey than the governor of Wormwood Scrubs.'

I was shocked: 'You mean he's a thief?'

They nodded in unison: 'Yes. But only to order. In that way, he says he cuts out the middle man.'

Said Cindy: 'And if you just happen to mention that you're short of something, the next thing you hear is the sound of a brick going through a shop window in Muswell Hill Broadway, followed by Ernie knocking on your door and asking to be paid in dirty five pound notes.'

Angie bit her lip, worriedly: 'This is not good, Cindy. If the police find him with stolen property, he's for the high jump.'

Said Cindy: 'Mind you, Ange, he could always plead insanity, couldn't he?'

Her sister nodded, sagely: 'Oh yes, he could always do that.'

Angie turned to me. 'Oh dear,' she said: 'Seems like you're up to your armpits in doggie-do, sunshine.'

Cindy forced a smile, patted me on the shoulder reassuringly and said: 'But not to worry. Even if the worst does happen, we'll still come and see you on visiting days.'

For a moment I contemplated grabbing my luggage and making a run for it, before Ernie, with the police hot on his heels, turned up on my doorstep. Even sleeping under a dust-sheet in the shambles of my apartment would be preferable to sharing a cell with a professional recidivist. It was only when they looked at each other, then exploded into peals of raucous laughter that I finally realised the delightfully wicked

Seymour sisters had, in what I understand to be the local *patois*, simply been extracting *le urine*.

Between giggles, said Cindy: 'If you could have seen your face! It was a picture, wasn't it Ange?'

'A picture. But he took it all in good part, didn't he, Cindy?'

'Oh yes. He took it in good part,' agreed Cindy: 'Goodnight sunshine.'

Then each planted a big kiss on my cheeks, picked up the plates and made for the door. Ernie arrived a few minutes later with a brand new portable radio, for which I paid him in cash. I didn't ask him where he'd got it from and to be truthful, I really didn't want to know. Ignorance, as the English are prone to say, is bliss.

MARCH

I T RAINED IN MARCH. While the English have long maintained that the month of March 'comes in like a lion and goes out like a lamb,' this March came in more in the shape of an incontinent tomcat rather than a raging King of the Jungle. Scarcely a day had passed since my arrival in Muswell Hill when the heavens hadn't decided to mimic a particularly busy Parisian *pissotière* topping-up the potholes along the Broadway with grubby-grey water.

Happily, however, by the end of the first week in March, *Moscrop & Son* finally finished their work and departed. Even so, I felt quite sad to be leaving the warmth and comfort of my little bed-sitter. And the Seymour sisters in particular.

While I had been totally unsuccessful in persuading them to regard me as a sex object, I had enjoyed their company and in the isolation of my newly-renovated apartment, I felt a sudden pang of loneliness. Even the presence of *Moscrop & Son* would have been preferable to no one at all, for during my frequent visits to check up on their progress, I had, after a while, begun to find their father-son exchanges quite entertaining. As the son plastered and the father supervised, it occurred to me that their roles should really have been reversed, if only because it soon became apparent that there was more to the tattooed Tarquin than had previously met the eye.

To my growing surprise, I found Moscrop junior not only an exceedingly good worker, but knowledgeable with it, as evidenced by one of their many exchanges:

'Tarquin?'

'Yes Dad?'

'Soon as you've finished that, go down to the van and - '

'It's outside, Dad. In the corridor.'

'What is?'

'The lining paper for the living room.'

'Ah. Then you'd better go and fetch the - '

'Already done it, Dad.'

'You've already done what?'

'Brung up the brushes, table and paste.'

'Now how did you know that I - '

'Stands to reason, don't it? Plaster's dry and the room's ready for papering. That is what we're going to do next, isn't it?'

Moscrop senior seemed less than pleased at his son's obvious ability to be one step ahead. Perhaps he felt it undermined his authority.

'Well yes,' he said, through semi-gritted teeth: 'I suppose we could make a start on the living room, but the fact is - '

'The fact is, Dad, unless we get the lining paper up by tonight, we won't be able to hang the wallpaper tomorrow. Which means that we'll have bugger-all to do except knock back the PG Tips - and you know how I hate hanging around all day. So what d'you want me to do after this?'

Moscrop pondered. Then finally: 'I reckon we should paper the living room.'

'Good thinking, Dad.'

Afterwards, in the kitchen, as Alfred Moscrop plugged in the kettle, I said:

'You've done a good job there, Mr Moscrop. Trained the boy well.'

Moscrop glowered: 'Weren't me. Got a scholarship to the Building Trades Institute, didn't he? Came out top of the class. Oh yes, he's smart all right. Too bloody smart for my liking. Can't tell him anything. And I'm his father. His boss. It's not right, is it? Makes me look a right berk.'

Once again, I was unfamiliar with the euphemism, but a little while later, on asking Monsieur Ernie the meaning of the word, his response was short and to the point:

'It's cockney rhyming slang, innit? For Berkeley Hunt.'

And when he went on to explain its origins in detail, the word did seem to sum up Moscrop senior admirably.

Once the Moscrops had left, my first task was to refurnish the apartment with something a little more acceptable. But before patronising *Reg's Repossessions* of Finsbury Park, as previously instructed by *Le Courrier's* accountants, I would obviously have to dispose of most of the old furniture, now stacked in the centre of the living room. And how did one do that? I wondered.

'Well,' said Malcolm Nesbitt, as we walked along Muswell Hill Broadway together: 'You could always have a garage sale.'

We had bumped into each other inside the local *pharmacie*, where I had gone to purchase some shaving foam and a new razor, my recently acquired electric shaver having caught fire and expired in a whisp of blue smoke the day before, which possibly explained why it had been such a bargain. Malcolm, as far as I could make out, was there to stock up with a fresh supply of bandages for his mother's leaking legs and when I told him of my problem he was confident that a garage sale was the answer.

'Of course, a car boot sale would be better. You get more people. But you'd need to hire a van for that and besides, this is the wrong time of the year for car boot sales.'

According to Malcolm, car boot sales were - and are - a particularly English phenomenon. During the summer, half the population, it seems, load their cars with the junk they had acquired during the previous year, drive to a school playing field, public car park or village green and sell these unwanted items to each other. The following week, those very same items would again be offered for sale at a different playing field, car park or village green. Over a number of years, such articles changed hands again and again, some re-purchased and re-sold by the original vendors several times over. When I asked Malcolm to explain the point of the exercise, he simply shrugged and said:

'Well, it's a day out, isn't it? Anyway,' he continued: 'Like I said, it's the wrong time of the year for car boot sales, so it'll have to be a garage sale.'

'But I don't have a garage.'

'Oh yes you do,' said Malcolm: 'Number six. Round the back. Goes with the flat. You're very lucky,' he continued, struggling with the carrier bag that contained enough bandages to double-wrap the mummified remains of Tutankhamen twice over: 'Garages are at a premium in Muswell Hill. Some people would give an arm, a leg, or anything else that came to hand, to have the use of a garage.'

I then recalled the large, rather rusty iron key that hung on a nail to one side of the kitchen door which had not fitted any lock in the flat and I resolved to inspect my newly discovered garage as soon as I got home.

'All you have to do,' said Malcolm, as we awaited the lift to take us to the fourth floor: 'Is put a card in the paper-shop window and pin a few notices to the trees along the avenue and, on the day, they'll be queuing up to put money into your hands.' He shook his head in wonderment: 'Some people will buy anything. Even clapped-out furniture like yours.'

The lift arrived and began to make its creaky progress towards our apartments. As we were about to go our separate ways, said Malcolm: 'Let me know the date and I'll give you a hand to shift the stuff.'

'Thank you. You're very kind.'

'Not at all.' And almost as an afterthought: 'And if there's any room left, perhaps you'd let me and mother get rid of some stuff of our own.'

'Of course.'

'Mother wanted me to give it to the Salvation Army, but I told her: "Why pick on the Salvation Army?" I said: "They've never done us any harm."'

He gave his now familiar vague little smile and walked off down the corridor. I entered my apartment, dumped my purchases, took the key from the nail beside the kitchen door and went to inspect my new garage.

◈

It took a great deal of effort to turn the key in the lock and pull open the twin doors of number six, in the row of eight adjoining lock-up garages at the rear of the apartment block.

As the first daylight in years illuminated the interior, it revealed, much to my astonishment, what I later ascertained to be a left-hand-drive *Peugeot 203* saloon, circa 1972, with French number plates. A thick mantle of dust covered the entire bodywork and all four tyres had long deflated. It seemed clear that this *Voiture Française* had not travelled the highways and byways of Muswell Hill, or anywhere else for that matter, for some considerable time. But closer inspection suggested that, for its age, the vehicle appeared to be in good condition. Nevertheless, even if the late Antoine Didier's *Peugeot 203* could be made roadworthy again, what was one to do with it? This was England and thanks to *les Anglais'* legendary *perversité*, they still insisted upon driving on the wrong side of the road, even though the rest of Europe - indeed, most of the rest of the world - drove on the right. Moreover, this was a left-hand-drive vehicle and, after years of driving on the right, a slight lapse of concentration on my part could well culminate in a head-on collision with a vehicle coming the other way.

But my first task was to get the car out of the garage to make way for the disposal of my old furniture, and on discovering a foot-pump in the boot of the vehicle, I managed to get enough air back into the deflated tyres to enable me to release the handbrake and push the car out of the garage and into the courtyard. Malcolm Nesbitt helped me to dispose of the many cardboard boxes full of empty wine, spirit and beer bottles stacked up against the rear wall of the garage, which had presumably been stored there by Antoine Didier, after he'd carefully assessed their contents for the benefit of *Le Courrier's* readers.

'I never knew Mr Didier had a car,' said Malcolm, as we returned from the local bottle bank for the umpteenth time:

'What are you going to do with it?'

'I've no idea,' I confessed: 'Have it towed away for scrap, I suppose. It can't be worth anything.'

'Oh, I dunno,' said Malcolm thoughtfully: 'Like I said, some people will buy anything.'

In the event, he was proved to be right. Well, half right. We held the garage sale the following Sunday and while, at the end of the day, I had not sold one single piece of furniture, Malcolm had successfully disposed of a large variety of items, including a rubber hot water bottle, a paraffin heater, a tin kettle, an old manual typewriter, a garden fork with one tine missing, a large quantity of assorted books ranging from *The Jobbing Builder's Guide to Cement, Lime & Gravel,* to what I assumed to be a homoerotic novel entitled *Broken Buttocks* and, quite unbelievably, a desk diary for 1997.

Much to my surprise however, the *Peugeot 203*, though not officially in the sale, was sold within the first five minutes for an astonishing two hundred pounds to an eager, oiled-stained passerby who, with the glittery-eyed fervour of a dedicated car fanatic, apparently spent all his waking hours repairing and refurbishing old vehicles, the more geriatric the better.

In France, of course - and in Provence in particular - when a vehicle has passed its useful life, it is sensibly abandoned by the roadside, pushed over a cliff into a convenient ravine or turned into a chicken coop. In England, however, it appears that there are countless ancient-vehicle enthusiasts with a mission to restore and exhibit them to fellow oil-stained obsessives at specialist car rallies throughout the country, one such rally being held in the grounds of Alexandra Palace every August.

I cannot say I was surprised at the lack of interest in my

furniture, despite Malcolm's assurances that "everything would go." As the last would-be purchaser cast an incredulous eye at what was on offer and went off with a bemused shake of the head, I closed the garage doors and went back to my apartment, having simply replaced the car and empty bottles with a pile of unwanted furniture. But at least I would now be able to visit *Reg's Repossessions* and choose some better *meubles* to make my life a little more comfortable.

∽∾

The following morning, with the unexpected £200 burning a small hole in my pocket, I took a W7 omnibus from the top of Muswell Hill to Finsbury Park railway station and walked the last few yards down Blackstock Road to the three-storey Edwardian building that housed *Reg* and his *Repossessions*. I had carefully consulted the well-thumbed copy of a London street map which I had discovered amongst my predecessor's papers, along with a handful of receipts from an establishment called *The Palm Beach Sauna & Massage Parlour* in the nearby Archway Road, each itemising the services of which he had availed himself - such as Full Body Swedish Massage, Unisex Sauna and the intriguingly cryptic *'Special Extra Services.'* At the bottom of the pile was the original French *livre de bord* - the log book of the *Peugeot 203* - which confirmed that it was, as I had suspected, a company car.

The small corner shop, which bore the name of the oft-mentioned Reg, was not very prepossessing, despite the grandiose sign above the door claiming it to be a furniture *Boutique*. I opened the shop door and began to edge my way through the mountains of chairs, tables, couches and sideboards piled one on top of the other, right up to the ceiling. As I did so, a disembodied voice came from behind a massive mahogany wardrobe:

'Yes?'

'May I speak to Mr Reg, please?'

There was a sudden snort of laughter, accompanied by a strange clicking sound and the voice said: 'That may be a little difficult. He's been dead for fifteen years.'

I paused to reflect upon the fact that since arriving in England, most of my conversations with the local inhabitants, while starting off quite normally, usually developed into an exchange bordering upon the surreal. And this conversation was to prove no exception. The owner of the voice, yellow duster in hand, finally emerged from behind the wardrobe in the shape of a large, heavily made-up woman in her mid-fifties, with a blonde wig, enormous earrings, a short black dress with a *décolleté* deep enough to rival *Le Grand Canyon* and a quite remarkable set of large, ultra-white dentures, which clicked as she spoke:

'Reg was my father. Left the business to me.'

'I see. Yes, well, I happen to be looking for some furniture, madame. And if you would be kind enough to show me what you have in stock...'

'What sort of furniture?' She reeled off a list of furniture items with the speed of a machine gun, her dentures clicking like demented castanets: 'Any of that lot interest you?'

I gave a Gallic gesture of helplessness and said: 'I'm sorry, but I didn't catch most of what you said. I'm not English you see and if you could possibly say it again, but a little more slowly...'

'A foreigner, eh? We get a lot of foreigners in here. My husband Albert was a foreigner. Well, when I say he was a foreigner I meant he didn't come from around these parts. He was a Geordie. Came from somewhere up North - Newcastle I think he said - but he may just as well have been foreign, because when we first met, I couldn't understand a word he said.'

'These Geordies,' I said, puzzled: 'They don't speak English?'

'Not the same sort of English we speak. Can't think how they understand each other.'

Intrigued despite myself, I asked: 'Then how did you communicate?'

'We didn't. Not at first. Mind you, it wasn't very difficult to work out what he was after, but when I made it quite plain that there was going to be none of that and especially none of the other until he'd learned to speak proper English, he was soon talking twenty to the dozen.' She paused. Then half to herself: 'He's been gone for five years, now.'

That seemed to require a sympathetic response and, as gently as I could, I said: 'I'm so sorry.'

She looked at me in some surprise: 'Why should you be sorry? You didn't even know him.'

'Even so, when one's nearest and dearest passes over...'

She gave a grim smile: 'Albert didn't pass over - he ran off with that little blonde french polisher we employed at weekends.' Her teeth clicked angrily at the memory: 'And if I ever catch up with the little cow...'

My curiosity aroused, I couldn't resist asking: 'You employed a French polisher? Where did she come from?'

She looked at me, blankly: 'Stoke Newington, I think. Why d'you ask?'

'Not France, then?'

'France?'

'Well, you did say she was a French polisher and as I also happen to be French, I couldn't help wondering...'

'Oh, I see what you mean. When I say a french polisher, I didn't mean a *French* polisher or I would have called her a *French* french polisher, wouldn't I?'

As surreal conversations went, this one had begun to get completely out of hand and, before it could go any further, I thought it advisable to change the subject:

'About the furniture...'

She nodded and composed her dentures into what she presumably believed to be an agreeable smile, but which, from where I was standing, merely resulted in a rather unnerving rictal grin.

'Well now,' she said, somewhat ambiguously: 'Let me show you all I've got.'

'All you've got?' I repeated, anxious not to misunderstand her yet again.

'Furniture-wise.'

'Ah. Yes. Right. Of course.'

I was pleased to discover that what she had in stock was more than adequate for my needs. The *Le Courrier's* accountants' research proved to be very accurate and the prices were most reasonable. The following day, a battered furniture van drew up outside my apartment block and within minutes, the new - or nearly new - furniture was sitting comfortably in my newly painted and decorated apartment. And for the first time since I arrived in England, I was beginning to feel at home.

'Are you going to have a housewarming party?' asked

Malcolm, as we queued up at the local supermarket check-out. I was there to re-stock the *fridgedaire* with the basic necessities, as most of the time, purely in the line of duty, I would be dining out at carefully selected hotels and restaurants in London and South East England, at *Le Courrier's* expense.

The items in Malcolm's shopping basket indicated he was there to stock up on a wide variety of herbal infusions, pre-prepared vegetarian dishes suitable for the microwave and numerous jars of a mysterious substance that was apparently made from what the label claimed to be a "vegetable yeast extract." Noticing my curiosity, on our way home Malcolm opened one of the jars to show me its contents and, from its smell and sticky-black consistency, I immediately assumed its purpose was to provide a poultice to help alleviate the watery flow from his mother's lower limbs. Malcolm appeared to find this extremely amusing and after his braying laughter had subsided, he informed me that it was for internal application only - ie: to be eaten. And by way of demonstration, he scooped a large finger full from the jar and transferred it to his mouth, with obvious enjoyment.

'Delicious,' he said: 'Especially on toast or cream crackers. Tell you what,' he continued: 'I'll bring a plate-full for your housewarming party.'

'It's a kind thought, Malcolm, but why would I want to have a housewarming party? Who would I invite? I only know you and your mother.'

'And little Alice, of course. '

'Oh yes, of course,' I said flatly: 'And little Alice.'

'She does like you, you know.'

'Your mother?'

'Alice.'

I ignored the implication and said politely: 'She does?'

He nodded: 'I can tell. By the way she always gives that funny little grin every time she sees you.'

I didn't like to correct him. That funny little grin was simply little Alice baring her teeth in a silent snarl, confirming that at the very first opportunity, she intended to bury those very same teeth somewhere about my person.

'But about your housewarming party,' he went on: 'Why don't you combine it with a Neighbourhood Watch meeting? One's about due and, if we hold it in your flat, it'd be a good way of meeting all your neighbours.'

Though I knew little or nothing about English Neighbourhood Watches and how they worked, it seemed that the regular meetings were hosted by each Watch member in turn, everyone bringing something in the form of food or drink. And, as Malcolm had said, it would be a good way of meeting other members of our little community - even the elderly couple with whom I'd shared a lift and a garbage bag on my very first night in Muswell Hill and who, no doubt, were still convinced that I had a serious personal hygiene problem. It would, I thought, be nice to become part of a community again, instead of spending the next few months in lonely semi-isolation.

'Very well,' I said: 'Would you arrange it?'

'No sooner said than done,' he said immediately: 'And I'll get mother to make a large anchovy, turnip and marmalade flan. She's known for her flans, is mother. Always experimenting with different combinations.'

I thanked him profusely, while making a silent vow to eat well before the neighbours arrived, bearing food, drinks and marmalade flans. In the event, it turned out to be a very pleasant evening. In a strange sort of a way.

❧

'I believe you French eat foxes,' said the angular, middle-aged Mrs Ballard from the first floor front, in a precise, cut-glass English accent that brought to mind a piece of chalk being dragged across a blackboard. She seemed to wear a permanent expression of total disapproval. About everything.

'Eat foxes? Not to my knowledge, madame,' I said, truthfully.

'Oh yes you do,' she insisted: 'I read it in a book. It even gave a recipe of how to cook one.'

'Which book was that?'

'Can't remember what it was called, but it was written by an Englishman who'd moved to the South of France. To some village in Provence.' She wrinkled her nose in distaste: 'Fancy eating foxes. Must taste utterly foul.'

She nodded in the direction of the centre table which now displayed a wide variety of food, drink and Mrs. Nesbitt's as yet untouched *incroyable quiche*: 'Almost as disgusting as that woman's anchovy, turnip and marmalade flan. She's quite batty, you know. And her son's as daft as she is.'

Within the space of a few minutes, Mrs Ballard had given me potted biographies - mostly unflattering and undoubtedly slanderous - of all those fellow residents who were now eating, drinking and chatting amicably with each other around my living room. She finally ran out of neighbours to defame and weaved through the crowd to refill her glass of what, from the label, appeared to be Nipponese *Sauvignon Blanc*, donated by Mr Yen from number 18 who owned a local sushi bar. At the same moment, the gnarled, gnome-like Mr Phipps from number 33 detached himself from the group around the improvised bar and sidled towards me. He looked over his shoulder, lowered his voice and said:

'What's the unmerry widow been telling you?'

'The unmerry widow?'

'Mrs Ballard. That's what we all call her. Just look at her. A face to curdle the milk. We reckon she must have finger-wagged her late husband to death.'

'Oh, we didn't talk about anything in particular,' I said tactfully: 'Though she does seem to have the impression that we French consume large quantities of roast fox, in the same way the English eat roast *boeuf*.'

'What's wrong with that?' he said unexpectedly: 'I've eaten a lot worse than that in my time. Especially during the war. Meat was so short, you were grateful for anything. Pigeons, hedgehogs, squirrels. My mother used to send me and my little brother out into Alexandra Park to bring home anything we could find.' For a moment, he looked quite nostalgic: 'Nothing like a nice baked hedgehog, if you know how to cook them.'

More out of politeness than interest, I said: 'And how do you cook them?'

As soon as I said it, I knew it was a mistake. For the next ten minutes, the carnivorous Monsieur Phipps launched into a blow-by-blow account of how best to prepare *sa Recette de Hérrison Alexandra* in graphic and gruesome detail, including the final coating of the unfortunate creature's prickles in a thick layer of wet mud.

'And after baking, pull off the dried mud and the spikes come with it.' He kissed the tips of his fingers in the manner of a well-known English food columnist and part-time film director and said: 'Historic.'

I was suddenly grateful for the fact that I'd eaten a good

deal earlier and looked desperately around the room for a way of escape, before he could insist upon giving me a detailed *recette* for braised dormouse. But with his glass now empty, he again lowered his voice and said:

'So don't take any notice of what Old Aspidistra Face says. You eat what you like and enjoy it.'

'Old Aspidistra Face?'

'That's what we call someone who's always looking out of her windows to find out who's coming and going, while pretending to clean them. The glass must be paper-thin by now. Excuse me.'

He moved back to the bar, giving Old Aspidistra Face a friendly neighbourly smile as he did so. As in all small communities, French or English, hypocrisy obviously ruled. The moment his back was turned, it was the unmerry widow's turn to sidle over towards me, lower her voice and say: 'What did that awful little man tell you?'

'Not a lot,' I said, as tactful as ever.

'I hope he didn't give you the recipe for roast hamster. It's just one of his fantasies. He hasn't eaten a hamster in his entire life.'

'It was for roast hedgehog, actually. The ones he found in Alexandra Park, during the war.'

'Rubbish. For one thing, when the war started, Alexandra Palace was turned into a prisoner of war centre. For another, he spent most of the war as an evacuee in Leighton Buzzard.' She nodded in Phipp's direction, tapped her forehead significantly and said:

'He's quite potty, you know.'

She then moved away to greet the Community Policeman, who had just arrived to give his regular update. Again, I paused to reflect upon the difficulties of conducting a normal conversation in Muswell Hill without it lurching into the totally bizarre. But then, I reasoned, perhaps it was just me and what would be regarded as somewhat grotesque in Ménerbes, such exchanges were considered to be quite normal in Muswell Hill.

The Community Policeman, to the obvious boredom of the assembled Neighbourhood Watch members, launched into what appeared to be a standard address which they'd all heard before, ending his crime statistical update with a smile and a humorously pointed:

'Now if any of you are wondering if that old *cliché* about local villains waiting until the local Watch members have vacated their homes to attend a meeting such as this before breaking and entering every other flat in this block, well, what can I say? It's an amusing idea but it just isn't true.'

'He always says that,' muttered Malcolm Nesbitt into my ear: 'But that's just what happened in Crouch End.'

The meeting broke up and as I ushered the guests off the premises, including Mrs Nesbitt with her still untouched anchovy, turnip and marmalade flan, I was not displeased with the outcome. I had met and socialised with many of my neighbours - including the aforementioned elderly couple who, after an initial sniff as they crossed the threshold, finally accepted that I did not need to be thoroughly fumigated - and I was now on nodding terms with most of the residents of my apartment block.

I was just about to double-lock the front door when the doorbell rang. When I opened it, to reveal a downcast Community Policeman, the first thing he said was:

'Naughty-naughty, sir. You should have had the chain on, like I told you.'

'I take it you left something behind,' I said.

'Not really. I just need to use your phone. The thing is,' he confessed: 'While I was talking to you lot, someone nicked my patrol car. And my handset was inside it.'

For some reason, when I related this to Malcolm Nesbitt, it seemed to give him a great deal of satisfaction. After his initial braying laugh, he said:

'A classic case of the biter bit, right? Oh yes indeed. Must tell mother. Enjoys a good laugh, does mother.'

It turned out that he and Mrs Nesbitt had little sympathy for any member of Muswell Hill's Finest who proved to be human and fallible. Or for anyone else who failed to live up to their exacting standards. Even so, they had been the first residents to attempt, in their own way, to make me feel welcome in Muswell Hill and I resolved to be as pleasant to the Nesbitts as they had been to me. I would even try to extend this to little Alice Nesbitt. From a distance, that is.

APRIL

I T DIDN'T RAIN IN APRIL. Not one, single, traditional April shower the entire month. To me, this was just another typical example of English perversity, be it the weather, politics, the euro, or driving on the wrong side of the road. But by the beginning of my fourth month in Muswell Hill, I'd fallen into some sort of personal and professional routine that seemed to be working. I spent most of my time visiting hotels, restaurants and *cafés* in inner and outer London - including such famous English restaurants as *L'Epicure de France, Le Caprice* and *L'Escargot* and, at the other end of the scale, certain motorway eating establishments - if only to forewarn those *Le Courrier* readers intending to travel by road in the United Kingdom why they should try to avoid the need for sustenance during their journey.

However, as Malcolm had said, my Neighbourhood Watch party did prove to be a good investment in terms of my introduction to and acceptance by our little community, soon evidenced by an invitation to a birthday party at number thirty-seven, occupied by two elderly ladies - one of whom was celebrating her seventy-fifth birthday. I had already been informed (with a sniff of disapproval) by the censorious Mrs

Ballard that both Daphne and Deirdre had once performed on the London stage, but on entering their apartment, I was unprepared for the many framed photographs that adorned almost every wall - each featuring a young and nubile Daphne or Deidre - or both - in various stages of undress.

'You're the first, Mr LaPoste,' said my hosts who, despite their advanced years, were still slim and remarkably pretty. They were both attired in elegant, knee-length dresses with impressive *décolletés* and, noting my initial surprise at the photographs on display, they chuckled.

'That's right, dear,' said Daphne: 'That's us. I'm surprised Betty Ballard didn't tell you about us. She doesn't approve of us, you see. We were exotic dancers.'

'Started off at the *Windmill* and went on from there.'

Even I had heard of the once legendary *Windmill* theatre, in the heart of London's West End. During the Second World War, the theatre had proudly and deservedly boasted that, despite the many air-raids, "We Never Closed" and, because of the nature of the theatre's cheerfully uninhibited offerings, this soon became humorously paraphrased into "We Never Clothed."

The *Windmill* was London's answer to our own *Moulin Rouge* and featured scantily-clad dancers and totally unclad *poseurs érotiques* who recreated famous paintings in the form of artistic tableaux, such as *Venus at her Ablutions* and *Nymphs at the Waterfall*. Other attractions included the obligatory ostrich-feathered fan-dancer, an energetic *Can-Can* by the entire company and the occasional hapless comedian whose impossible task it was to entertain the mostly male, mostly grubby-raincoated audience with non-stop patter, while they waited impatiently for the *Windmill* girls to change their G-strings and make their next appearance.

'Why thank you, dear,' said birthday girl Daphne as I presented her with one of the few remaining bottles of Antoine Didier's *Cognac*: 'I love brandy. Got a taste for it when I was going out with a French chap.' She turned to her friend: 'You remember him, don't you Deirdre? The one who picked me up in *The Moo Cow Milk Bar* just around the corner from the stage door. What was his name, now?'

Deirdre sighed: 'How would I know? You were always being picked up in the *Moo Cow*.' To me, she said: 'That's where we all used to go. After the show. The thing was, after doing six performances a day, all you wanted was a cup of hot milk and a good night's sleep.'

Daphne snorted with amusement: 'Not that we used to get much of that.'

Said Deirdre primly: 'Yes, well, that was a very long time ago. When we were both young and foolish.'

'Weren't we just?' said Daphne, suddenly wistful: 'And wasn't it lovely?'

For a moment, Deirdre looked just as wistful, then nodded:

'Yes, it really was.' To me, she said: 'Of course, there comes a time when you have to move on and when Daphne and I were offered a tour with an animal act, we decided to leave the *Windmill* and go on the road.'

'We were the original *Nudes in a Lion's Cage*,' said Daphne proudly, pointing to a photograph which featured both her and Deirdre in a tasteful pose on each side of a lion's cage, in which squatted a rather woebegone lion looking blearily towards the camera.

Said Deirdre: 'Oh yes. We toured all over England with Leo and Arthur.'

I nodded: 'Leo being the name of the lion, of course.'

'No dear,' said Daphne patiently: 'That was Arthur. Leo was the lion tamer. Started off running a flea circus but got fed up with being bitten.'

By now, I had developed a sixth sense about conversations that were about to lurch into the bizarre yet, despite myself, I said: 'But wasn't he afraid of being bitten by the lion?'

'He was bitten. Lots of times. He wasn't much cop as a lion tamer. But as Arthur didn't have all that many teeth left, it never caused any lasting damage.'

'Besides,' said Deirdre: 'He was stoned most of the time.'

'The lion?'

'The trainer.'

'Well, both of them, actually,' corrected Daphne: 'Leo on gin and Arthur on tranquillisers.'

'Ah,' I said, silently chiding myself for aiding and abetting yet another trip into Never-Never land. My hosts went on to explain that the act required them to pose artistically on the top of two tall plaster pedestals within the lion's cage, attired in nothing more than the odd goose-pimple or two. The aged, dentally-challenged and heavily sedated Arthur was then pushed into the cage and the girls had to maintain their motionless, highly artistic poses while the animal clawed unenthusiastically at the pillars while the audiences supposedly held their breaths.

'The thing is, you see,' said Daphne: 'In those days there was a Lord Chamberlain - a sort of censor - who only allowed nudity on stage if the artistes never moved a muscle. It wasn't a bad job. A bit boring, but quite well paid.'

This time, it was Deirdre who gave a sudden snort of amusement: 'It wasn't very boring that night at the *Stockport Theatre Royal*. You remember, Daphne? When Leo got legless and forgot to give Arthur his shot?'

Daphne shuddered: 'Remember? How could I forget? I've never been so petrified in all my life.'

I was beginning to enjoy their cheerful reminiscences. They were a great deal more entertaining than Malcolm's blow-by-blow accounts of his mother's weeping legs. From what I could gather, on that fateful evening at the *Theatre Royal*, Stockport, when the lion was finally pushed into the cage without its nightly injection it was suffering from severe withdrawal symptoms and a momentous hang-over. On looking up and perceiving the first fresh meat it'd seen in months, the animal apparently decided that, as *steak tartare* seemed to be on the menu, this was its opportunity to improve its diet.

Roaring and snarling as it had never roared and snarled for years, it reared up on its hind legs and clawed at the pedestals on top of which Deirdre and Daphne were posing so artistically. When the pedestals started to rock and sway, the girls were obviously presented with somewhat of a dilemma. While Arthur was unlikely to inflict any serious injury, the animal's claws could do untold damage to the career prospects of anyone who made a living posing in "the altogether," as the girls quaintly described it. And the question was - to move or not to move? To defy the Lord Chancellor and reach for the upper bars of the cage and swing there, legs kicking, totally in the buff, as the English say - until help arrived?

Daphne, the consummate professional, merely gritted her teeth and refused to move a muscle. Deirdre, on the other hand, was obviously more into self-preservation than appeasing the Lord Chamberlain and dropping into a less-than-artistic crouching position, she wrapped her arms and legs around the pedestal, her bare *derrière* twinkling merrily in the direction of the audience and howled: 'Get the bloody thing out of here!'

Said Daphne: 'Of course, the audience thought it was all part of the act and started to applaud. I mean, at that time, someone doing acrobatics in the nuddy was quite a novelty.'

And Deirdre said: 'But that's when we decided we'd had enough of show business, didn't we Daphne? So I married my pork butcher from Leeds and Daphne married her accountant from Croydon. They'd been chasing us for years. Daphne and I always kept in touch, though.'

Asked Daphne: 'Have you got a young lady, Mr LaPoste?'

'Not at the moment, no.' There seemed little point in clouding the issue by mentioning that I still had a wife.

Said Deirdre: 'Then we'll have to find you one, won't we Daphne?'

'We certainly will. Everyone needs someone. When our husbands died, Deirdre and I decide to move in with each other. Of course, it's not the same as having a man about the house, but at our age, what would we do with one, anyway?'

Deirdre gave another snort of amusement: 'I'd think of something.'

It was very easy to like the ex *Danseuses Éxotiques*. They had so much *joie de vivre* and during the course of the evening, I began to wonder if they were really serious about finding me a young lady - and if so, whom.

The doorbell rang. The other guests were starting to arrive.

༚༚

'What are you doing on Saturday?' asked Daphne and Deirdre, when we met by chance in the lift, the following day.

'Um... nothing, as far as I can remember.'

'Then come for dinner. There's someone we'd like you to meet.'

'Oh? May I ask who? Or should I say whom?'

'Say it any which way you like,' said Deirdre.

'Just be there,' said Daphne: 'Seven o'clock sharp.'

Their years of working together as a theatrical double-act had obviously resulted in an unspoken *rapport* similar to that of Siamese twins and the following Saturday, at seven o'clock sharp, I duly presented myself at the door of 37, a bouquet of carnations in one hand and a bottle of *Jack Daniels* in the other, which had been on special offer at the local branch of the well-known London wine merchants who called themselves *Oddbins*.

Why any wine merchants would wish to present themselves as odd, strange or even faintly peculiar was beyond my comprehension and I simply put it down to the English *penchant* for galloping eccentricity.

'Well thank you, dear,' said Daphne: 'You love *Jack Daniels*, don't you, Deirdre? Got a taste for it when you were going out with that American GI. The one who picked you up in Piccadilly Circus during the blackout.'

'He didn't pick me up,' said Deirdre coldly: 'We just sort of bumped into each other. In the dark.' To me, she said: 'Come in, Mr LaPoste. Help yourself to a drink.'

The dining room table was set for four places and, just as I was wondering who was destined to make up the quartet, the doorbell chimed the first four bars of *There's No Business like Show Business*.

'Good, that, isn't it?' said Daphne, cheerfully: 'Reminds us of our mis-spent youth.'

Deirdre had already gone to answer the door, returning a few moments later with the missing guest - a well-scrubbed young woman in her late twenties, attired in a plain, rather baggy knitted dress that owed nothing to fashion and which successfully concealed what was inside it. Her so-called sensible shoes, more suitable for a woman twice her age, completed her ensemble and I could not help feeling a trifle disappointed at her appearance. While the girl was certainly not unattractive, with huge brown eyes and masses of chestnut hair, now primly tied back into a large bun, I had been hoping to meet someone a little less... spinsterish. Or someone who promised to be what my Crouch End acquaintance would have called "a bit of a goer." A younger version of Daphne or Deirdre, in fact.

'This is Angela,' said Deirdre.

'And this is Mr LaPoste,' said Daphne.

As Angela looked shyly down at the floor, I took her hesitantly-proffered hand and brushed it with my lips, as I was sure my hosts expected me to do. I was right.

'Oo-er,' said Deirdre approvingly: 'See that Daphne? How very French of you, Mr LaPoste.'

'Pierre, please.'

Said Deirdre, as she poured the girl the requested glass of tonic water: 'Angela's my niece. On my late husband's side. But more like a daughter, really. There was no fruit of the union, you see.'

'Pardon?'

Angela appeared to blush prettily and said: 'I think Aunt Deirdre means that she and Uncle George had no children of their own.'

'Me and my late Oliver, neither,' said Daphne: 'And it wasn't for the lack of trying. But at the end of the day, our husbands couldn't even father a ferret.'

'Time for dinner,' said Deirdre and disappeared into the kitchen.

As we took our places at the table, said Daphne: 'I hope you like roast pork, Mr - er - Pierre.' She gave Angela a wicked little grin and continued, quite deadpan: 'We know the French much prefer fox, but there's not much of it about at this time of year.'

'Take no notice of her, Pierre,' said Deirdre as she emerged from the kitchen with the standard English starter of prawn cocktail and thin brown bread: 'She overheard barmy Betty Ballard going on about it at your Neighbourhood Watch party.'

I looked across the dining table towards the demure Angela who was looking steadfastly into her prawn cocktail, without even the flicker of a smile at Daphne's little joke. It was going to be a long evening.

'Angela's a librarian,' said Deirdre: 'She runs the library at *St. Catherine's School for Girls*, in Highgate.'

Of course she does, I thought, ruefully. While I've known a few comely librarians in my time, one who dressed as badly as Angela and had the demeanour of a frightened bush-baby would seem to indicate that she had led a very sheltered life and would only feel secure in the fusty, dusty world of a school library. Though grateful for my hosts' attempts to try and find me a female companion during my stay, I was surprised that they obviously thought I would consider the frumpish Angela even remotely attractive. However, the dinner progressed quietly and pleasantly enough, with Angela occasionally joining in the conversation but adding little of interest. At the end of the evening, at the request of my hosts, I agreed to escort Angela back home to her flatlet in nearby Highgate - although common courtesy dictated that I would have volunteered to do so anyway. On seeing us to the door, Daphne and Deirdre kissed Angela maternally on the cheek and exchanged a knowing look.

Said Deirdre: 'Now you behave yourself, Pierre. We all know what you French are like.'

Angela seemed to blush once again: 'Really, Auntie Deirdre. I'm sure Mr LaPoste will be the perfect gentleman.'

'Of course I will,' I said, from the heart.

Said Deirdre: 'I was only joking, darling.' To me, she said: 'My niece is too shy by half, Pierre. Needs someone to bring her out of herself.'

The lift arrived. It contained three other residents, also on their way down to the main entrance. I ushered Angela inside, nodded politely towards the others and the lift doors closed. Which is when I felt an anonymous hand discreetly but firmly squeezing my left buttock. I looked at the other residents in surprise and alarm, then at Angela, who was staring straight ahead, her *visage* quite without expression. When the lift finally came to a halt and the other residents moved out into the hallway, Angela turned towards me and, without the hint of a smile, said:

'Nice bum. Your place or mine?'

Said Angela, the following morning: 'I always dress like a refugee from Oxfam when my aunt asks me for dinner.'

She was sitting in what her aunt would have called "the nuddy" on the end of my bed. Her metamorphosis from shrinking violet to *femme fatale* in the few seconds it had taken for her to shed her clothes, was mind-boggling. Her previously camouflaged figure had turned out to be quite *Rubenesque*, with an ample bosom, generous curves and long, shapely legs. Her un-bunned hair now cascaded around her shoulders like a golden cape and Angela, in a few short seconds, had become a cornucopia of all things prurient.

'They've been trying to marry me off for years, that's why I always try to make a bad first impression. I mean, you won't believe the men they've come up with. They've even tried to team me up with that dip-stick from number 42.'

'Malcolm,' I said automatically. While I was unfamiliar with the expression, it did seem to fit Malcolm like one of his hand-knitted gloves.

'That's him. But I like my own space. My independence. I haven't the slightest desire to end up in a Muswell Hill semi-detached, with a boring husband and a clutch of screaming kiddie-winkies.'

I was relieved to hear that. While I've always considered myself to be an enthusiastic and energetic *amoureux*, after just one night of sexual gymnastics in the company of Deirdre's exceedingly demanding niece, I was feeling totally debilitated and had come to the conclusion that if, like Monsieur Ernie, from The *Savoy Private Guest House*, I wished to continue to have a body to call my own, a protracted relationship with the uninhibited Angela would be most inadvisable.

'Well, best be off,' she said abruptly, reaching for her clothes: 'I'm due at the *Colney Hatch Health Club* at ten o'clock and my personal trainer hates to be kept waiting.'

For what? I thought, although I could hazard a guess. In the event, my guess was not all that far out, for as I was showing her off the premises, she gave a sly little smile and said:

'Ever done it on a trampoline?'

'Can't say I have, no.'

'You should try it. Beats the hell out of an interior sprung mattress.'

With that, she reached forward, gave my *compteur d'eau privé* a friendly squeeze and took the lift down to the ground floor, where (I later discovered) on emerging from the main entrance, she had looked up to see the beady-eyed Betty Ballard pretending to clean her windows, suspicion writ large across her face. Obviously in a buoyant frame of mind, Angela had given the resident Aspidistra Face a bright smile - and a single finger.

Mrs Ballard's reaction was not recorded.

Much to Daphne's and Deirdre's disappointment, I made no attempt to see Angela again and she made no attempt to contact me. Her personal fitness trainer obviously possessed what I did not - a trampoline.

'Ah well, said Deirdre philosophically: 'What wasn't meant to be, wasn't meant to be.'

'We'll just have to find him someone else,' agreed Daphne: 'Someone who looks a bit more presentable. I love the girl dearly, but she really should try to do something with herself. Yes, Pierre needs someone with a bit more go in her.'

A bit more go in her? *Mon Dieu.* I paled at the thought.

The rest of April passed quite uneventfully, with the sad exception of the demise of the elderly widower who had occupied number 27. Although I had never actually met the man (he had been too indisposed to attend my Neighbourhood Watch party) I and the rest of the residents were obviously expected to pay our last respects to the late member of our little community. Thus the following morning, I joined the other mourners in the chapel of rest at *Jeremiah Unsworth & Sons, Funeral Directors & Monumental Masons, Established*

1897 (as it proclaimed in gold lettering over the funeral parlour door) in nearby East Finchley.

It was my first experience of an English funeral, which turned out to be non-secular. Old Mr Messiter apparently had a deep-rooted hatred of organised religion whatever its persuasion and many an unfortunate Jehovah's Witness, Moony or Mormon who'd had the temerity to knock upon his door had been frozen in mid-solicitation by a colourful and highly inventive stream of personal abuse.

The chapel was quite full and the eulogies even fuller - apart from the less-than-fulsome address by Malcolm Nesbitt, who was clearly out of his depth.

'What can one say about dear old Jim Messiter?' he began: 'He wasn't one of us, of course - he came from somewhere oop North. Lancashire, I believe.' He adopted what I assumed to be Malcolm's idea of an authentic Lancashire accent: 'Aye. Real 'ecky-thump country, as they say - '

He paused to allow his audience to chuckle if they so wished. They didn't.

He continued: 'But he soon fitted in with us Muswell Hillbillies. And why? Because of the sort of man he was. And what sort of man was that, you may ask. Well, for one thing he was certainly... er...' He paused: 'And there again...'

Another pause. Malcolm's mind had obviously become a complete blank. While his mother glared at him from the front row, he looked up towards the ceiling in search of inspiration, but obviously didn't find any.

He tried again: 'And, well, I'm sure no one who knew Jim as well as I did would deny that above all else, he was... er... well, you know.' By now, he was getting desperate and he looked around the chapel for a little help, but simply met the stony faces of the assembled mourners who were shifting uncomfortably in their seats, presumably waiting for the orations to end and the deceased to be interred, followed by an invitation to partake of the traditional Northern English post-funeral fare of port wine and seed cake.

Malcolm ploughed on relentlessly: 'I've got so many happy memories of old Jim, it's difficult to know where to start. But if I could sum up his long and successful life in one short sentence - '

It was old Jim's younger brother, down for the funeral from 'ecky-thump country, as Malcolm called it, who summed it up for him. From the back of the chapel, he bawled:

'He were a good speller at school. Now let's get him planted.'

And that was it - apart from the port wine and seed cake. There was none of the pomp and ceremony of a French funeral, with its horse-drawn hearse, weeping relatives and enough food and wine to feed most of Provence. When we all returned to the dear departed's empty apartment, it was even emptier than when the late Mr. Messiter had finally left it, his relatives having already denuded it of anything of value prior to departing back "Oop North" with their spoils.

Said Mr. Phipps, as he munched his way through a piece of seed cake:

'You do know what old Jim said he wanted on his tombstone, don't you?'

'I'm afraid not.'

For the first time since I met him, Mr. Phipps actually smiled:

'He wanted: "CHEERS JIM, ALL THE BEST, THE NORTH LOST A GOOD 'UN, WHEN YOU WENT WEST."'

This time, Mr. Phipps actually chuckled out loud. While I was aware that traditionally, the Northern English did have a reputation for graveyard humour, as did the peasants of Northern France, I was at a loss to understand what was so amusing about this particular example. Perhaps it was the way he said it. Even though by now, I was fairly fluent in basic English, I obviously lacked the knowledge to recognise the subtleties, the nuances of English *patois* and I resolved there and then to do something about it, possibly via a local language school.

'I mean,' continued Mr. Phipps: 'You can't help but laugh, can you?'

Oh yes I can, I thought. Easily.

The end of April came a day later and as an English spring was now well on its way, it was time, I thought, to go shopping for more summery attire.

How wrong can one be?

MAY

IT WAS BITTERLY COLD IN MAY and the local *gendarmarie* came and arrested my window-cleaner. The two happenings were not directly related but they did impinge upon each other, if only because the rainless April had allowed the frequent deposits from Muswell Hill's many incontinent flying pigeons to remain firmly adhered to most of my windows - like *merde* to a *couverture*, as we say in Ménerbes.

But the strange case of the itinerant window-cleaner was to reach its *dernière* a little while ahead. For me, the month began when I awoke on May Day, to discover what, according to Malcolm Nesbitt, was "brass monkey weather." I wasn't at all sure how a monkey, brass or otherwise, fitted into the equation, but after turning up the central heating to the maximum, I abandoned all thoughts of refurbishing my limited wardrobe with the aforementioned summery apparel and resolved to buy a fisherman's jersey instead.

As I stood shivering at the bus shelter for a number 102 to take me to the Brent Cross shopping centre, a few miles down the road, I reflected upon the traditional English optimism about the weather when planning annual events. I had plenty of time to do so. As expected, the bus was running late and the moving electronic sign within the shelter which displayed a report of the 102's progress was, as usual, a monument to misinformation. While one could not help but approve of any attempt by the transport companies to inform their customers when they might expect their bus to arrive (in order for them to decide whether or not to shiver in discomfort or hail a passing taxi), the accuracy of the information was invariably somewhat *imprévu* and I couldn't help thinking - a little uncharitably, perhaps - that if the electronic sign had worked, with typical English perversity, the service would have been withdrawn immediately.

Still reflecting upon the ambiguities of life and living in England, I remembered what my guidebook had said about that first day of May. The date apparently held a very special place in the English calendar - particularly in the more rural areas - when, for centuries, with the sap officially risen, the young villagers had celebrated the advent of spring by dancing around a maypole on the village green, each holding a long coloured ribbon with which they formed a pretty design on the vertical maypole (which presumably represented a multi-coloured fertility symbol) before pairing off into the nearby woods with a flagon of rough cider and a laudable determination to ensure the survival of the species.

Again according to the guidebook, one of the great English rural traditions on May Day was, on retiring the previous evening, the most comely maiden in the village would sing a little song which began:

"Wake me early, mother dear, for I'm to be Queen of the May."

In recent times, however, while the traditional song is still performed, it appears that after frequent accusations of sex-discrimination by equally pretty village *hommes*, the honour of being chosen to be Queen of the May is now open to both genders. Or all three, as it were.

To the less romantic and more political, the first of May is, of course, also somewhat of an oxymoron called Labour Day when, in homage to the admirable traditions of honest toil, many workers fail to turn up for work.

As I continued to ponder upon life's little contradictions, I suddenly perceived a man on a bicycle pedalling along the Broadway, an expanding ladder on his shoulder and a plastic bucket on his handlebars. I hailed him urgently. When he came to a halt, I politely inquired if he was, by profession, a window-cleaner. He looked at me, sighed wearily and said:

'No guv. I'm the bleedin' Archbishop of Canterbury, ain't I?'

'*Pardon?*'

'Course I'm a window-cleaner. Why d'you think I ride around with a bucket on my handlebars? In case I get caught short?'

As the English are well known for their fondness for irony, I assumed he was just being ironic and merely asked him if he'd care to clean my windows.

'When?'

'Now, if you wish.' The jersey could wait.

'Where are you?'

'Where am I?'

Another weary sigh: 'Where's your gaff?'

'My gaff?'

His eyes narrowed: 'You foreign?'

'Yes.'

He nodded: 'Thought so. Where d'you live?'

'France.'

'Jesus. Where d'you live around here?'

'Oh. Just round the corner. Arcadia Court.'

'Arcadia Court?' He looked worriedly about him and shook his head: 'No, sorry, guv. Can't help you.'

'Why not?'

Again he looked nervously about him and said:

'I had a very unhappy experience at Arcadia Court and I swore I'd never go back there again.'

'What sort of experience?'

'Let's just say that a certain lady in the first floor front came on a bit strong, all right?'

I was somewhat taken aback: 'Mrs Ballard?'

'I didn't wait to ask her name.' He was about to pedal off: 'So like I said - '

'Wait,' I said: 'She's not at home at the moment. She helps out at a charity shop on a Thursday.'

'You sure?'

'That's what she told me. Besides, with me around...'

He thought for a moment, glanced at his watch then nodded: 'All right. I'll fit you in right now. Before her at 29 Micklethwaite.'

And an hour or so later, he had cleaned all the windows of my apartment, both inside and out and had accepted my offer of a cup of tea. His claim that Mrs Betty Ballard, the tight-lipped widow of the first floor front had "come on strong" with him was, to me, both bizarre and highly amusing. If it was true then, like many highly-moral people, Mrs Ballard obviously had a pronounced, if carefully concealed, appetite for original sin - though why on earth she had decided that my window-cleaner was a suitable target for her carnal desires was totally mystifying.

Aged around 40, small of stature and with a permanent air of morose resignation, he hardly seemed capable of raising little more than a smile. So what, I wondered, could she have possibly seen in him? Unlike the legendary Casanova, he didn't even have big feet. He seemed to read my mind and said, sorrowfully:

'It's the job.' He sipped his tea, drew deeply on his hand-rolled cigarette and continued: 'Every window-cleaner's greatest professional hazard. And it always starts the same way. You're going about your business, cleaning the windows of a regular customer, doing no harm to nobody, when this woman from across the road spots you from her bedroom window. And they always say the same thing.' He adopted a falsetto female voice and said: 'Yoo-hoo, window-cleaner? When you've done Mrs Beasley, will you do me, too?' He sighed: 'A reasonable enough request, you might think. But you'd be wrong - that's just the beginning. Cos a couple of minutes later it's: "Would you like to do the insides, first? You can start at the top and work your way down."' He shuddered at the memory: 'You can imagine the rest. And it's always the same sort of woman.'

'And what sort is that?'

'Widowed and willing. Or unwed and still wondering.' He shook his head wearily: 'I'm not saying they're bad women. Not for the most part. Just lonely, that's all.' And half to himself: 'Yes, it's sad to see what loneliness can do to a person.'

'But surely, Mr... er...'

'McPhee. Angus McPhee. No. Hold on. Liversedge. Sid Liversedge - I mean Perkins. Yes, that's it. Harry Perkins.'

The man was so exhausted, he was obviously having difficulty in remembering his own name.

'But surely... er... Mr Harry, you could always tell these ladies you're too busy and say no.'

He looked at me in genuine astonishment: 'Say no? And lose a customer? I've got a living to make, for God's sake. Besides, you never know for sure what she's after until you've got your shammy-leather out.' He rose to his feet: 'Thanks for the tea, guv. See you a fortnight Thursday?'

'Yes. Please.'

He took a deep breath: 'I'll just do her at 29 Micklethwaite and call it a day.'

He didn't elaborate on what was expected of him from her at 29 Micklethwaite and I didn't ask. But it would make an amusing anecdote for the delightful Daphne and Deirdre next time they came to dinner.

ༀ

I travelled to the shopping centre the following day and duly bought my fisherman's jersey. And that was my first mistake. I donned it immediately and for the first time in forty-eight hours, I felt genuinely warm. Too warm, in fact. For on the way home, the sun suddenly burst into view and by the time I had stepped off the bus in Muswell Hill Broadway, I was, as Mr. Phipps would say, sweating cobs. By now, I should have realised that the celestial *Clerc des Temps* was playing yet another little game with the weather and wondered why he always seemed to pick on the English with whom to amuse himself. I sweated even more when I opened the door to my apartment which, with the heating having been on at full blast for the last 24 hours or so, was now giving a fairly accurate impression of *l'enfer de Dante*.

I went to turn it off and did so. Or rather, tried to do so, as unfortunately, the dial of the thermostat, when turned, came neatly off into my hand. There seemed only one thing to do.

Turn off the radiators individually. Looking back, this turned out to be my first experience of what the English call "sod's law," for though I managed to turn off two, the valves of the other six radiators around the apartment were jammed solid with decades of white paint - as was the supply valve to the gas boiler lodged under the sink. I realised then that there was only one option still open to me. After a slight hesitation, I reached for the telephone and tapped in the number of *Alfred Moscrop & Son, Master Builders, Painters & Decorators.*

And that was my second mistake of the day.

☙❧

'You're very lucky, squire,' said Alfred Moscrop, as predictable as ever, when I finally managed to contact him through his mobile phone: 'We're already working in the area.'

'Whereabouts in the area?'

'Right here. Arcadia Court. Flat 27.'

I thought for a moment then remembered that number 27 was the late Mr. Messiter's place and had been empty since his demise.

'Oh? Who's the new tenant?'

Through the phone came the sound of a distant howl, followed by the crash of what sounded like a falling ladder.

'Hold on,' said Mr. Moscrop as he obviously turned to address the source of the disturbance: 'Tarquin? You all right?' There was a muffled groan, then a muttered: 'Yeh. Think so.' Bawled Moscrop senior: 'What did I tell you about climbing ladders with a bucket of paste in each hand? What did I tell you? You could have done yourself a hurt.' To me, he said: 'He's all right. He landed on his head.'

'About my central heating. When can you come and take a look at it?'

The sound of teeth being sucked dubiously, then: 'Hard to say, squire. Me and Tarquin are up to our necks at the moment - hold on.' Once again he addressed the unfortunate Tarquin: 'Don't just lie there, son. Go and put the kettle on.' To me, he said: 'It's all go here - but since you're an old customer, I'll try and nip up sometime today. All right? Right.'

Telephonic communication was abruptly terminated and, reluctant to spend the rest of the day in what had become - even with the windows open - more of a sauna than a sitting room, I decided to drop my spare keys into number 27 and ask Mr Moscrop to inspect my central heating at his leisure, while I went into London to find another restaurant to review.

'How are your bowels?' asked little Mr Phipps, abruptly.

'My bowels?' I said, somewhat surprised, until I realised that with his pronounced South London accent, what he said was not what he meant.

'I assume you mean "bowls,"' I said: 'The game your Sir Francis Drake played on Plymouth Ho-Ho before sailing off to fight the Spanish Armada.'

'Bowels, yes. What did you think I meant?' said the ever-testy Mr Phipps: 'And it was on Plymouth *Hoe*. Not Plymouth *Ho-Ho*. He was a sailor. Not Father-frigging-Christmas.'

'Yes, well,' I said: 'I've played some *boules* occasionally in Ménerbes - but I don't think it's anything like your bowls. Why do you ask?'

I was again waiting at the bus-stop at the Muswell Hill

roundabout - this time in pleasantly warm weather - he for a number 102 to take him to the shopping centre and myself for a number 134, which would take me in the direction of Tottenham Court Road - and more particularly, to nearby Charlotte Street, the home of several small but reputedly good restaurants. Mr Phipps, it transpired, was a member of a local bowling club and in need of a new pair of rubber-soled shoes, in readiness for the start of the outdoor bowling season in late spring or early summer.

'Weather permitting, of course. And if you fancy a game,' he continued: 'I'll take you along and show you around the club-house.'

'That's very kind of you.'

'Not really. We could do with some new blood. Some of the older members usually drop off their perches during the winter, so there are always plenty of vacancies.'

My knowledge of English bowling clubs was strictly limited, though I did recall that while I was on my first visit to England all those years ago, when sipping a glass of depressingly warm beer in a London hostelry, I had witnessed a fierce argument between a couple of bowling enthusiasts on the merits of what appeared to be the two different kinds of games, namely lawn green and crown green bowling - the main distinction between the two being that the former was seemingly performed on a totally even lawn and the latter on a lawn that was a little higher in its centre. I have to confess that the point of the argument entirely escaped me, as in all other respects, the two games appeared to be identical.

When I mentioned this to Mr Phipps, his reaction was one of mild outrage:

'Identical?' he echoed: 'There's no comparison. Crown green bowling is what they do up North. And d'you know why they do it? Because it's easier, that's why. All you need is brute force and ignorance. It's got none of the subtlety and finesse of lawn green bowling.'

From which I gathered that Mr Phipps was an *aficionado* of lawn green bowling. He warmed to his theme:

'Crown green's almost as bad as indoor bowling. That's what they play inside those buildings that look like tram-sheds - there's one in Highgate, just over the hill. And they don't even play on grass, for God's sake. They play on plastic! Yes, plastic! Can you believe it? And why? Just so's they can play all year round, that's why.'

By now he was quite red in the face. I had obviously hit a nerve.

'After all,' he continued: 'What could be better than *The Belvedere Bowling Club* on an English summer's day, with the men in their blazers and flannels, the ladies in their white dresses and sun hats - and the gentle click of wood against wood as they kiss each other at the far end of the green?' He thought for a moment, then added: 'The balls, I mean.' He nodded with utter conviction: 'Oh yes. There's nothing quite like being a Lawn Ranger - and come summer, I'll prove it to you.'

'A Lawn Ranger?'

'That's what we call ourselves.'

'Ah,' I said.

'As in the Lone Ranger and Tonto.' He looked at me expectantly: 'It's a sort of joke. A play on words.'

'Ah.' I said again, still unable to think of a suitable response.

Fortunately, at that very moment, the number 102 bus pulled up in front of us and the sprightly Mr Phipps was driven off in the direction of the shopping centre.

I wasn't at all sure that I wanted to become a member of a club that appeared to appeal mostly to those of advancing years, as I had been advised by my travelling acquaintance from Crouch End that one of the best ways of meeting young, unattached and semi-attached *jeunes filles* was to join a local tennis club.

In the event, I didn't feel the need to join either. But that decision was some time ahead.

⦿⦿⦿

Said Alfred Moscrop: 'What did I say to you about this central heating? What did I say?'

'You said whoever put it in needed locking up.'

'I said whoever put it in needed - oh, you remembered. You'll have to have a new one, you know.'

'A new what?'

'Boiler. This one's clapped out. I can fit new valves in the radiators, but I wouldn't even try to repair the boiler. Timer's gone, piping's dodgy, thermostat's knackered and the seals are falling apart.'

Dodgy? Knackered? While I'd got the drift of what he was trying to tell me, my limited knowledge of English *patois* did put me at a distinct disadvantage when dealing with local tradesmen and I resolved once again to try and find a language school which would provide some assistance in that direction.

Said Moscrop impatiently: 'So what's it to be, squire?'

My somewhat feeble response, was:

'Are you sure I need a new boiler? It was working well enough until today.'

'Yes, well, that was before my inspection, wasn't it? I had

to dismantle it to give it a proper going over and it dam' near fell apart in my hands. All it's good for now is a skip.'

I surveyed the remains of the boiler which now littered the kitchen floor and cursed myself for not being around for his so-called "inspection." And now it was too late. But at least the warmer weather was upon us and the need for central heating was hopefully receding with each passing day.

'Very well,' I said, wearily: 'How much and when?'

While I knew "when" would merely be any date right off the top of Mr Moscrop's balding head, I had to go through the process for the sake of *Le Courrier's* accountants.

'Well now...'

Out came the notebook and pencil stub and the muttered calculations began, followed by pursed lips and a sad shake of the head:

'I'm afraid it's going to cost you, squire. What with the basic unit, the extra parts, pipework and, of course, the labour. And we mustn't forget the VAT, must we?'

We mustn't, obviously. But the thought of trying to find to find some one else at such short notice had little appeal and it was, after all, a classic case of the devil you knew. He gave me the figures, snatched a date out of thin air and departed for flat 27, turning in the doorway for:

'Oh, just one thing. I've had to turn the gas off at the mains, so that'll mean no heating, hot water or cooking for a few days, all right? Right.'

No, it wasn't all right but I had no choice. As I switched on the electric percolator for a strong *café noir*, I wondered where I could possibly go for my daily *douche* while the new boiler was being installed. I could, I supposed, take advantage of the facilities on offer at *The Palm Beach Sauna & Massage Parlour*, so regularly patronised by the late Antoine Didier.

But at that moment in time, I had no desire for either a unisex sauna or any of the "extra special services" - whatever they were. Thus a simple shower would doubtless turn out to be prohibitively expensive.

I wondered if I should prevail upon the Nesbitts for the use of their bathing facilities - and dismissed the idea immediately, having had a sudden vision of being cornered naked in the bathroom by a vengeful Alice, teeth bared, intent on savaging my defenceless *accessoires personnels*.

The irritable Mr Phipps, with his regular flights of fancy? I didn't think so. I had no wish to be a captive audience while he pontificated on the finer points of his beloved bowels.

And certainly not the (allegedly) sexually predatory Mrs Ballard. My late father once told me (and he should know) that in any *histoire de coeur*, the vital factor was opportunity. Thus it would be most unwise of me give the unmerry widow of *Arcadia Court* the opportunity to ravish me in the privacy of her first floor front.

That left only one - or rather two - of my neighbours who might be of help to me in my situation *difficile* - Deirdre and Daphne. In anticipation of a favourable reply to my request, I decided to invite them out to dinner at one of the better local restaurants. It was Deirdre who answered the telephone:

'Of course you can use our bathroom, dear. Any time you like.' She giggled: 'If you're lucky, we might even scrub your back for you. I'm glad you rang. We were just talking about you. Can you come to dinner tomorrow night? There's someone we'd like you to meet.'

I could not help but smile. So the indefatigable and original *Nudes in a Lion's Cage* were still trying to find me a suitable lioness.

'That's very kind of you,' I said: 'But it's my turn to take you to dinner. And please bring your friend.'

I reserved a table for four at a small local restaurant for the following evening, one which was regularly patronised by Deirdre and Daphne and I couldn't help wondering if the "someone they wanted me to meet" would be as... exotic as Angela had turned out to be.

He was.

❧

'Binkie's a dancer,' said Daphne: 'Well, he was, a long time ago.'

Said Deirdre: 'He was at the *Windmill* the same time we were, weren't you, darling?'

'I certainly was, dear heart,' said Binkie, nibbling delicately on his corn-on-the-cob: 'And what bonar days they were, too.'

Daphne gave a snort of laughter: 'Bonar days? No one says bonar any more, you silly old tart. That's pure 1950s.'

'Yes, well, I'm a child of the '50s. We all were.' To me, he said: 'Please forgive my friends, Pierre. But whenever you get three old pros together, it's always the same - a gay little trip down old memory lane.'

Gay was the operative word. Binkie Baxter was the first transvestite I'd ever met - let alone dined with - and I was finding it a very interesting experience. He was nothing like the image I'd always had of a typical cross-dresser, which was one of brightly-coloured silk dresses, high-heeled shoes and blonde beehive wigs. He had obviously chosen to eschew the flamboyant and outrageous and wore a tasteful, well-cut, designer black dress, minimum jewellery and little or no make-up.

Despite his advancing years, he was still slim of figure with a dancer's long legs and delicate, unlined hands. One could, in a phrase, take him anywhere - as both Deirdre and Daphne obviously did.

'We've always kept in touch,' said Daphne, adding wickedly: 'And we wanted you two to meet because we think you could be good for each other.'

'Now you just stop that,' said Binkie severely: 'Just look at the poor man. He's gone as white as a sheet.' To me, he said: 'What the naughty little cow meant, was - if you need a regular cleaner, we need regular clients. When I left the business, in nineteen hundred and whoops-a-daisy - '

'Whoops-a-daisy?'

Said Deirdre: 'That's just his way of hiding his age, Pierre. Vain as a peacock. Always was.'

'Pea-hen please, darling,' corrected Binkie coldly. To me, he said: 'As I was saying, when I'd danced my last *fandango*, so to speak, I opened this domestic agency - our offices are in Tufnell Park which is quite close by - and as I gather you live on your own, the girls thought you might be in the market for our services. If you haven't already made other arrangements, of course,' he added quickly.

Said Daphne: 'His people are very good. All resting actors. And as we like to do our little bit for anyone in show business, we just thought you might be interested.'

I was. While I was quite capable of keeping my apartment reasonably clean and habitable, after a hard day's eating, drinking and writing, domesticity had long since lost its appeal. Binkie and I agreed on the first of June for one of his cleaners to call and the three of them then got down to the serious business of exchanging theatrical reminiscences.

'I bumped into Beryl O'Sullivan the other day,' said

Binkie: 'You remember Beryl. The pretty little Irish girl who couldn't see a thing without her glasses.'

Said Deirdre: 'Oh yes. We remember Beryl. Nice girl. The three of us were quite close at one time, weren't we, Daphne?'

'Very close,' confirmed Deirdre: 'The punters loved her. *The Windmill Commandos* in particular.'

It appeared that the *Windmill Commandos* was the name given to the members of the audience who, at the end of each show, clambered commando-like over the seats in front of them in an attempt to occupy any recently-vacated front-row seats, especially when it was the myopic Beryl O'Sullivan's turn to do the fan-dance. And for very good reason.

'The thing is, Pierre,' explained Daphne: 'When you do the fan-dance, you're supposed to use your ostrich feathers to cover up your - pardon my French - itchy-kitchy-coo when you turn towards the audience.'

'And the problem with Beryl,' said Deirdre: 'Was that she was not only blind as a bat, she had no sense of direction, either.'

'And as a result,' said Daphne, with another snort of laughter: 'The Commandos knew that when Beryl was prancing about on stage, they'd always get an eyeful of her little feather duster.'

Little feather duster? *Itchy-kitchy-coo*? Did they really talk like that in the 1950s?

Said Daphne: 'When we tried to tell her, she said that we were just jealous because she got so much more applause than we did.'

'Which, of course, she did,' said Binkie: 'And for the very same reason, presumably, she also got herself a very rich husband.'

'Oh?' said Daphne, looking slightly put-out: 'I didn't

know that.'

Binkie nodded: 'I ran into her coming out of *Harrods*. With enough carrier bags to open her own department store.'

'Never!' said Deirdre: 'Ah well,' she said to Daphne, philosophically: 'We didn't do too badly ourselves, did we Daphne?'

Binkie chuckled: 'You would have done even better, my darlings, if you'd flashed *your* little feather dusters once in a while.'

Said Daphne with a sniff: 'Crafty little cow. We never liked her, did we Deirdre?'

'Never,' said Deirdre.

In show business, memories seemed to be a moveable feast. The reminiscences, mostly scandalous, often libellous but certainly entertaining, continued well into the evening. After Binkie Baxter had departed by mini-cab for Tuffnell Park, I escorted "the girls," as Binkie had called them to their door, politely declining a nightcap and/or a late night shower. It had been an interesting evening. And once again, I found myself wondering if the "resting" actor (which I gathered was a euphemism for being unemployed) whom Binkie would delegate to clean my apartment, would be as *piquante* as Binkie himself.

She was.

❦

The following Thursday afternoon, on returning from London's West End after a professional visit to an establishment presided over by noted English chef Marco Pierre White, in order to assess his culinary skills for the benefit of *Le Courrier's* readers (which, I should add, I found most acceptable - his essentially English *Aile de Raie aux Câpres et Pommes Vapeur Française* in particular), I was confronted with my window-cleaner, who had been patiently waiting for me outside *Arcadia Court* for access to my apartment. After he had completed his window cleaning, on returning to his bicycle, he found the police patiently waiting for *him*. He was remanded in custody until the following month and out of sympathy for his predicament, I agreed that when the time came, I would act as a character witness, even though all I really knew about his character was that he appeared to be honest and hard working.

All in all, it had been an interesting month and towards the end of May, not only had Alfred Moscrop successfully installed my new boiler and departed, the imminent arrival of Binkie Baxter's actor-cleaner on the first day of June was extremely fortuitous. As usual, the state of the kitchen after Moscrop's labours left much to be desired and what was now required was a complete spring-clean.

In the event, I got a little more than that. A spotless apartment and the beginning of a very interesting relationship.

Pierre LaPoste

JUNE

I ROSE EARLY ON THE FIRST OF JUNE, which turned out to be a delightful day, for more than one reason. The sun was shining. The spring and early summer flowers were in full bloom in every public open space, from Alexandra Park to Hampstead Heath and the gardens of so many houses in the numerous residential avenues around Muswell Hill were ablaze with colour. Although there was a small private garden behind *Arcadia Court* for the benefit of the residents, being on the fourth floor, all I had was several empty window boxes sitting forlornly on my window ledges, shamefully neglected by the late Antoine Didier and which all cried out to be rehabilitated.

Thus, in the company of many like-minded local residents, I strolled down Muswell Hill and turned left into Springfield Avenue, walking past the well-kept *jardins* of this pleasant *cul-de-sac* towards the narrow public footpath, which served as a shortcut to the local Gardening Centre and Alexandra Palace itself. The English obsession with gardens and gardening - and smooth grass lawns in particular - has long been a source of wonder to the French who have sensibly, if indolently, preferred to rely upon nature to provide the local flora and fauna, rather than spend a small fortune on grass-seed, fertiliser and gardening equipment in order to produce a pristine, beautifully manicured sward to rival those of their neighbours.

Since mid-May, on each and every evening and especially at weekends, through my open windows had come the distant hum, roar and clickety-clack of electric, petrol-powered and manually-operated lawnmowers, mixed with the occasional howl of anguish from a distraught *jardinier* as he came upon a single strand of crab-grass.

The Garden Centre was well stocked with a bewildering variety of plants suitable for a window box and after making my selection, I arranged to have them delivered, along with several bags of compost, the following day. On the way home, I met Malcolm Nesbitt taking the same route to Alexandra Park, where, he told me, he intended to spend the afternoon bird-watching. He was certainly dressed for the part, with a pair of powerful *lunettes* - binoculars - slung around his neck, a waterproof anorak over his arm and a small haversack which, he told me, contained a flask of tea and a packet of sandwiches prepared by his mother.

'What sort of sandwiches?' I inquired roguishly, recalling his mother's adventurous, if not universally popular, anchovy, turnip and marmalade flan: '*Rosbif* and raspberry preserve?'

He looked at me blankly: 'Roast beef and jam? That's gross.' For a moment, he looked quite nauseated: 'One bite and I'd throw-up. Besides, we don't eat meat. You know that.'

It was obvious that my admittedly feeble attempt at humour had gone right over his head and I hastened to reassure him. I was too late.

'If you must know,' he confided: 'They're cheddar cheese

and custard.' It was my turn to feel nauseated: 'Mother's very creative with leftovers,' he continued: 'And while they may not be to everyone's taste, they really do go down a treat.' He actually licked his lips at the thought: 'Well, must be off. Got to find a place to hide in the long grass, before all the other twitchers get there.'

'Twitchers?'

I searched his face for any signs of a nervous tic but found none.

'That's what they call us bird-watchers.'

'Why?' I asked, waiting for an equally incomprehensible reply.

'No idea,' he said cheerfully: 'They just do, that's all - so TTFN and see you around, no doubt.'

One day, I promised myself, I would actually meet a relatively normal Englishman and have a relatively rational conversation. But this was obviously not going to be the day. *TTFN? Twitchers*? It really was time for me to find a language school and I resolved to do so, without further delay. Malcolm gave a little wave of the hand and strode off in the direction of Alexandra Park.

Sadly, it transpired that on this occasion, his attempt to observe his feathered friends was not a success. It seemed that no sooner had he settled himself down in the long grass and raised his binoculars to scan the surrounding parkland, the first local wildlife that had come into range was an energetic young courting couple who had also taken refuge in the long grass for their *alfresco* activities. Unfortunately, his protestations to the irate young couple that he was no *voyeur* had fallen upon deaf ears, resulting in Malcolm having to limp home nursing a bloody nose and a particularly colourful black eye. It is then that he wisely, if reluctantly, came to the conclusion that if he was to avoid any similar misunderstandings, it might be advisable for him to hang up his binoculars and take up fretwork, instead.

Which he did.

෴

The doorbell rang just as I had finished washing the dishes, prior to the imminent arrival of my new actor-cleaner. Like my late mother, who invariably felt the need to clean the entire house before the arrival of her daily help who, of course, had been hired for exactly that purpose, I also felt the need to make the place look reasonably neat and tidy beforehand, if only to avoid frightening my new cleaner away.

The large, rather formidable lady of indeterminate age who swept into the flat had the appearance of a Spanish galleon in full sail.

'Maggie Turnbull,' she announced briefly in a loud, rasping voice that I later learned was the consequence of many years of performing in provincial theatres, where every thespian was required to be clearly heard in the last row of the upper circle, without the benefit of a microphone. She was dressed in a shapeless summer dress that reached down to her ankles and sturdy, thick-soled boots which she proceeded to remove before rummaging in her voluminous handbag for a pair of carpet slippers.

'Can't scrub floors in my Doc Martens,' she explained: 'They leave marks everywhere. Now. Where d'you want me to start?'

'Anywhere you like, Madame.'

She nodded, pulled a colourful apron from her bag, wrapped it around her substantial waist and headed for the kitchen, where she attacked the grimy evidence of Alfred Moscrop's last visit with an efficiency and determination that was most impressive and which must have had every sensible dust-mite fleeing the premises.

By the time she had finished, the apartment was barely recognisable from the one I had inherited from Antoine Didier and after switching off my computer, I insisted that she should take a rest and partake of a cup of *café*.

'Most kind.' But as I turned towards the kitchen, she held up a imperious hand and said: 'No. I'll make it. You carry on with your work.'

She disappeared into the kitchen, emerging a little while later with a large mug of black instant coffee which she sipped while replacing her slippers with what she called her "Doc Martens.'' As she tightened the laces, she said:

'They may look a bit butch, but they're so comfortable.' She paused, gave me a knowing smile and said: 'I suppose you're wondering why my face is so familiar?'

'Er, no,' I said truthfully: 'I assume you're an actress, but as it happens - '

'I was the matron in *General Hospital*. Y'know, on television - '72 to '78 - and before that, I toured in Sailor Beware in the late Peggy Mount's role, God bless her.'

'No. I'm sorry. The thing is - '

She was obviously extremely disappointed.

'How about *In Loving Memory*, then? That TV sitcom about a north country undertaker with Thora Hird? God bless her, too. I played her business rival. You must have seen that.'

'The fact is, madame - '

'*The Bill*, then. A couple of years back. I played the old - the middle-aged lady standing at the bus stop with a bag of oranges. Only a cameo part, but everyone said I still made quite an impact.'

'I'm sure you did, madame, but the last time I saw television was in France. Over six months ago.'

'France? Oh, of course, you're French, aren't you? Binkie told me. No wonder you don't remember me.' She seemed quite mollified and gave me a nervous little smile:

'I was beginning to think you didn't like my work.'

In show business, as in the writing profession, the self-esteem of an actor or writer was, as Daphne and Deidre once put it, as fragile as a fairy's fart.

'On the contrary Madame,' I said reassuringly, indicating the gleaming apartment: 'I'm more than satisfied with your work. In more ways than one.'

'Well thank you.' Another little smile: 'And it's Mademoiselle. Never been married. Never seemed to find the time from the moment I joined *Frank H. Fortesque's Famous Players* in Manchester as a very young assistant stage manager. Not that I didn't have the chance,' she continued somewhat defensively, as though challenging me to think otherwise: 'Oh dear me, no. You may find it hard to believe, but I was quite pretty as a young girl.' She was silent for a moment: 'Pity in a way. That I never married, I mean. Especially now acting engagements are so few and far between. I love housework, you see. Yes, really. And cooking. It's so different from being an actress. So... relaxing.'

She rose abruptly to her feet, thrust out her hand and shook mine heartily:

'You will phone Binkie, won't you? To say you're happy with the way I did things.' Another doubt: 'You are happy, aren't you?'

'Very happy, Miss - er, Mizz Turnbull.'

'Miss, please. Mizz sounds like a fizzy drink. But in your case, it's Maggie.'

'Pierre.'

'Thank you. See you next week?'

'I'll look forward to it.'

She strode out into the corridor and moved towards the lift.

So large. So full of life. And so vulnerable.

The Word Perfect School of Languages was just off Colney Hatch Lane, a few metres along from Muswell Hill Broadway. It had, apparently, been established in the late 1970s to cater for the linguistic needs of the huge influx of foreign *au pairs* who had arrived in their hundreds to take care of the children of Muswell Hill's upwardly-mobile, middle-class couples who, after a miscalculation of the fertility cycle - or a faulty condom - had found themselves with unexpected progeny and desperately needed help to maintain their standard of living.

I had finally found the time to attempt to improve my knowledge of colloquial English, but as I climbed the creaking wooden stairs of the old red-brick building - which had once probably housed a single Victorian family and a host of domestic servants - I almost forgot what I was there for. It was difficult to remain single-minded with dozens of exuberant, nubile and often extremely pretty young women brushing past me on their way to their language classes. Swedish accents mingled with German, Dutch, Czech, Polish, Spanish and others too esoteric for me to identify. Male students were in a minority. In fact there were none at all, as the local council, I later learned, had decreed some years earlier that only female *au pairs* would be allowed to look after local children.

I then realised that it was quite possible - even likely - that I would be the only male in the class, but far from feeling like Adam in the Garden of Eden, surrounded by not just one, but a multitude of Eves, I began to question the wisdom of trying to learn the subtleties of a foreign language under such distracting conditions.

On reaching the office of the principal, my doubts were suddenly magnified as, when I explained why I was there and what I hoped to learn, the large, cheerful, middle-aged man behind the desk nodded vigorously and, with a German accent as thick as a large slice of *Gateau Battenburg*, said jovially:

'The English *patois* is that what you wish to learn, ja? Hokey-Dokey. Nein problem, old fruit.'

I looked at him in some surprise. I had expected, not unreasonably I believe, that anyone purporting to be an English teacher would at least be fairly fluent in the language. Unless, of course, he was merely the school administrator.

'You really do have someone familiar with the English vernacular, local idioms and idiosyncrasies?'

'Sure ting.'

'Then who would be my tutor?'

'Me.'

'You?'

'Ja.'

Which is when, as we journalists say with monotonous regularity, I made an excuse and I left, after having embarked on yet another fruitless journey into the surreal. I consoled myself with the notion that if I could find a book on the subject, it would not only be more rewarding, but a good deal cheaper, too.

❧

As I entered *Arcadia Court* on my way back from the Muswell Hill bookshop which, with admirable simplicity, traded under the name of *The Muswell Hill Bookshop*, I was confronted by an emerging Mr Phipps, dressed in a smart blue blazer with brass buttons and grey slacks with creases which looked sharp enough to cut through solid steel. He was carrying a leather holdall in which, from its shape, I assumed he accommodated his set of bowls. He halted, gave me a brief nod and said abruptly:

'Open night. *The Belvedere Bowling Club*. Saturday next. I'll pick you up at seven o'clock pip-emma. Okay? Okay.'

Before I had a chance to reply, he was gone.

The doorbell rang at precisely seven o'clock the following Saturday evening and as I hadn't been able to think of a suitable excuse for refusing his invitation, I reluctantly accompanied the eager Mr. Phipps to his beloved bowling club, situated behind nearby Queen's Avenue, in time for the last few matches of the day. I had to admit that on a balmy June evening, it was very pleasant to sit on the veranda of the club-house, sipping a quite acceptable Chilean *Chardonnay*, while watching the neatly-dressed players attempting to place their bowls as close to the smaller jack as possible.

Mr. Phipps finished his game and joined me:

'Drinks on him,' he said somewhat smugly, nodding towards his defeated and downcast opponent who was walking towards the club-house bar: 'Fancies himself as dab hand at the game, but he'd be better off playing marbles. Doesn't know one side of a wood from the other - its all in the bias, you see. Get that wrong and it's straight into the gutter.'

I didn't ask for a translation. I merely surveyed the peaceful scene, sipped my *Chardonnay* and said, quite sincerely:

'I have to say, Mr Phipps, this is all very civilised. Unlike other, more strenuous sports, it is so... restful to watch a game totally devoid of violence, bad language or one player fouling another.'

Phipps looked at me sharply: 'Are you serious?' He answered himself: 'Yes, I suppose you must be, being French and not knowing the game and that.' He lowered his voice, leaned towards me and said: 'Course there's fouling. Goes on all the time. Bad language, too. And as for violence...' He indicated an elderly player who, by his posture, appeared to be both arthritic and rheumatic and who was standing, bowl in hand, close to his half-crouching opponent who was about to make his play.

'See the old feller? Never loses a game. Not that he's all that good, but what he lacks in skill, he makes up for in other ways. Watch.'

As he spoke, the heavy, solid plastic bowl (even though it was still apparently called "a wood") seemed to slip from the elderly player's fragile fingers to land fairly and squarely on his younger opponent's foot. The latter gave a howl of agony, sank to a sitting position on the grass and started to massage his toes, obviously in genuine pain.

The old man seemed visibly distressed and desperately apologetic:

'I'm so sorry, Henry. I really am. It just sort of slipped out my hand. My damned arthritis again. Never know when it's going to give me a twinge. You all right? Haven't broken anything, have you?'

It was an impressive performance and if Mr Phipps hadn't

forewarned me, I would have thought the old man's concern was genuine. His opponent was not so sure:

'You silly old bastard!' His voice echoed around the green: 'You did that on purpose, because you were one game down.' He groaned again: 'And if you weren't such a stupid old fart, I'd stuff your bowls where the monkey stuffs his nuts!'

The old man looked extremely hurt: 'Did it on purpose? That's a terrible thing to say. But if that's what you think, I'll give the match to you, here and now.'

'Oh no,' said his opponent, struggling to his feet: 'You're not going to get off that easily. I'm going to win fair and square. Now stand back.'

He sent his bowl curving towards the distant jack. But the damage had been done. In his pain and anger, the player's finely-tuned bowl control had obviously gone all awry and his bowl ran silently past the jack to drop neatly into the gutter. His howl of rage was even louder than before:

'Oh bugger! Bugger-bugger-bugger! That was all your fault, you geriatric old git!'

The other players on the green turned to look at him, reprovingly. The old man gave them an apologetic gesture and said: 'I did offer to give you the game.'

'Shut-up and play!'

'If you say so.'

The old man crouched to deliver his bowl, with just the hint of a smirk on his face, which both Mr Phipps and I couldn't help but discern. Phipps turned to me with a mocking smile and repeated:

'No violence, no bad language and no fouling? You don't know the half of it.'

He chuckled: 'At times, it's even dirtier than croquet - and that's supposed to be the dirtiest of the lot.' He seemed extraordinarily proud of the fact: 'That's what makes the game so interesting. So why don't you join the club?'

'I'll think about it,' I said untruthfully. I'd already thought about it and had failed to see where the enjoyment lay in being maimed by elderly English psychopaths on a pleasant summer's evening at *The Belvedere Bowling Club*, all in the name of recreation. What had happened, I wondered, to that legendary English sense of fair play - historically encapsulated in that well-known phrase: "it's just not cricket." Did it ever exist? Or had it always been a popular misconception actively encouraged by the English Establishment to lull the rest of the world into a state of false security? While it may have existed on the playing fields of Eton, it certainly wasn't much in evidence on the playing green of *The Belvedere Bowling Club*, Muswell Hill, on a Saturday evening in June.

When I finally informed Mr Phipps of my decision, he seemed both surprised and disappointed. But even though, as he had once said, his club was keen to see new blood on the green, I had no wish for it to be mine.

For his first courtroom appearance, I was not called to act as character witness for Harry Perkins, my window-cleaner. He was brought before the local magistrate merely to establish, in English legal parlance: "If there was a case to answer." There was, it seemed. And Harold Perkins, alias Sidney Liversedge and Angus McPhee was sent for trial on a charge of serial bigamy. The police, it transpired, had decided to arrest the accused after investigating the contents of an anonymous letter, postmarked Muswell Hill, presumably from one of the many

Pierre LaPoste

women whose advances had been resisted by the already over-extended window-cleaner. Her from *Arcadia Court's* first floor front, I wondered? After all, anything was possible.

It was interesting to compare the French and English legal systems. In France, a *Juge d'Instruction* would assess the case and if it was appropriate, the accused would be sent *en Correctionnelle*. In England, the accused would be sent from a local Magistrates' Court to a Crown Court, where he would be tried by a judge and jury. Thus towards the end of June, Harry Perkins duly appeared in the dock and was asked if he pleaded guilty or not guilty to the charges.

'Oh, guilty, your honour,' he said immediately: 'Oh yes. I'm guilty all right. No doubt about it.'

I wasn't the only one who was rather surprised at the defendant's reply. The judge, the jury of "twelve good men and true" as the English say (which happened to include three women) - plus Perkins' barrister and solicitor, also seemed to be rather bemused by their client's eagerness to incriminate himself. As were Mrs Perkins, Mrs Liversedge and Mrs McPhee. The three middle-aged women were all totally different in size, shape and appearance and all sat side by side, each dabbing her eyes with a handkerchief and each looking tearfully and accusingly towards their shared *l'homme de la maison* in the dock.

'And by the way, your honour,' continued Perkins: 'The name's Finnegan. My real name, I mean. Freddie Finnegan.' To his counsel, he said: 'Meant to tell you, but it sort of slipped my mind.'

The elderly judge looked at him in genuine astonishment. As did most of the court.

'Are you telling the court that there is a Mrs Finnegan, too?'

'That's correct, your honour. Married ten years and never a cross word.'

He looked up towards a small, bird-like woman in the public gallery and gave her a little smile. She smiled in return and blew him a kiss. The other women turned as one and glared venomously in her direction.

The judge and the clerk of the court exchanged a look of utter incredulity.

Said the judge: 'Purely as a matter of interest, Mr - ' He looked down at his notes - 'Mr Finnegan, is it?'

'Finnegan, yes. That's the one, sir.'

'Purely as a matter of interest, would you please tell the court why you went through a form of marriage with all these women?'

Finnegan looked surprised at the question:

'D'you think I wanted to, your honour? D'you think I enjoyed moving from house to house, wife to wife, every night of the week? D'you think it was easy trying to pretend to the others that I had a second job on the night-shift to explain why I wouldn't be home that evening? And there's the other thing, isn't there?' He made a gesture of despair: 'Sometimes, I couldn't even find the strength to wring out my shammy leather.'

'Even so,' said the judge, carefully: 'I'm still somewhat confused. How on earth did you manage to run four separate establishments on your take-home pay as a window-cleaner?'

'I didn't, your honour. None of them are short of a few bob, you see. Own their own houses, money in the bank. Investments. They never asked me for any money and they never got none. The only one I did support was Gloria.' He nodded towards the woman in the gallery: 'The wife. The real one,' he added, for clarification.

Said the judge: 'That still doesn't explain why you considered it necessary to marry the other three. Why did you?'

Finnegan seemed quite surprised at the question:

'Well, I mean, it stands to reason, your honour.' He turned towards the jury and said earnestly: 'I could hardly expect them to live in sin, could I?' He indicated the three women and continued: 'These are all good, decent people. And in a small community like ours, if it became known that their window-cleaner was just their... well, their toy-boy, think of all the gossip, all the shame, all the humiliation. And none of them deserves that. They're not bad women. Just lonely, that's all.'

The ageing toy-boy's logic, let alone his social conscience, was impeccable and the spontaneous burst of applause from both the public gallery and the jurors had the judge reaching for his gavel. When order had been restored and the jury had gone through the formality of returning a guilty verdict, he gave his judgement:

'Frederick Finnegan - '

'Frederick *George* Finnegan, sir - '

'Frederick *George* Finnegan.' He made a note: 'Thank you. You have been found guilty of the charges against you and even though all the women involved have refused to make a formal complaint against you and as it appears that there were no children from your various liaisons, you shall go to prison for a maximum of two years, one year suspended.'

Finnegan looked at him in disbelief: 'Twelve months, your honour? With good behaviour, I'll be out in a few months! That's no good to me! He became incensed with rage and disappointment:

'Don't you understand, you old tosser? I need the rest. The recuperation.' He turned to his counsel, pointed towards the judge and demanded: 'Tell the old twat he's got to give me at least three years. I deserve it. I need it.'

By the stunned silence throughout the court, it would appear that this was the first time in English legal history that the accused had demanded a longer sentence than the one the judge had decided was appropriate. However, for his contempt of court, the Old Twat - an epithet with which I was unfamiliar - obligingly increased Finnegan's sentence by a further six months (also suspended) and my erstwhile window-cleaner was led down to the cells, still protesting vehemently at the inequity of British justice.

My day in court had been an interesting experience, though I was surprised at the severity of the sentence. In France, bigamy - multiple or otherwise - is not thought to be a particularly heinous crime, for two main reasons. The first being that far from taking advantage of the women involved, it was considered that in most cases, the bigamist was merely trying to spread a little happiness among the lonely and deprived. The second reason is more pragmatic. Any *Juge* worth his gavel would have come to the conclusion that the miscreant had already been punished enough.

After all, in Finnegan's case, he had ended up with four mothers-in-law.

❧

JULY

IT RAINED IN JULY. Not seriously. Just enough to give some much-needed liquid nourishment to the lawns and flowerbeds of Muswell Hill. The first few days of the month had been warm and sunny and, despite the well-known vagaries of the English climate, the local council and business community had bravely embarked upon their annual celebration of all things bright and beautiful in one of London's more salubrious suburbs. Known as the *Muswell Hill Festival*, each end of the nearby Fortis Green Road, just off of the Broadway, becomes closed to motor traffic to allow the street to be turned into a bunting-bedecked pedestrian area and market-place, with dozens of stalls lining the pavements, selling everything from food to fancy goods, books to baked potatoes, poetry to pottery.

The street entertainers usually include (or so I was informed) an over-amplified local rock band, clowns, face-painting instructors, several guitar-wielding buskers competing with each other to *assassinés* Bob Dylan, plus the obligatory chain-saw juggler who, unfortunately, at last year's festivities, appeared to have been somewhat out of practice and had to be rushed to hospital to have a thumb and forefinger sewn back on, much to the delight of the crowd, who thought it to be all part of his performance.

As I strolled around the various stalls, I enjoyed the carnival atmosphere and mixing with the local residents, while sampling what was on offer from the stalls and ice-cream vans. The mood of the festival was cheerful and friendly. It reminded me, on a much smaller scale, of the weekly market back in the Lubéron town of Apt and for a moment, I felt that familiar pang of homesickness. I wondered how my house had fared during the winter months and as I was due for some home leave, I resolved to take a short trip to Ménerbes as soon as possible. The following weekend seemed fairly clear and due to the ease of travel to Aix via the *Eurostar*, I decided to book my tickets the following morning.

But it was not to be. Like the organisers of the *Muswell Hill Festival*, Malcolm Nesbitt, an equally compulsive organiser, was also prepared to gamble on the possibility that the good weather would continue for some time and for that reason, he had decided to assemble his barbecue equipment which, with my permission, had been stored in my garage. The same day, all the members of the Residents Association received a hand-written invitation to join him and his mother to dine *alfresco* the following Sunday, in the little private garden behind *Arcadia Court*, where there was a patch of grass just large enough to accommodate such a social gathering. His invitation was couched in such friendly terms, it was difficult to turn it down and I postponed my visit back home until a later date.

In England, I later discovered, eating *alfresco* was a relatively recent phenomenon and despite the unpredictability of the English weather, British holiday makers returning from package *vacances* on the Costa del Sol and other warmer, drier climes where beach barbecues were part of the package, had developed a taste for outdoor eating and had invested in the equipment necessary to produce the traditional English *alfresco* fare of blackened sausages, scorched drumsticks, frozen (on the inside) hamburgers and beef-steaks with semi-cremated exteriors but red, raw and dripping with gore in the centre.

July and August, it seemed, were the months when, at the first sign of a rainless day, the smoke from a thousand barbecues would spiral upwards from Muswell Hill's patios, gardens and public places, polluting the atmosphere and forming a menacing cloud over Alexandra Palace.

This was reminiscent, I was told, of the time not so many years ago when, before the passing of the what became known as *The Clean Air Act of 1954* (arguably the most environmentally-friendly legislation since Queen Victoria had allegedly demanded that breaking wind in public should be made a criminal offence), London had been colloquially known as "The Smoke."

The Nesbitt's barbecue was very much a communal affair. Tables and chairs from various apartments had been assembled on the grass and the guests sat watching Malcolm with interest as he struggled to ignite the charcoal with lighter fluid, without losing either or both of his eyebrows.

As on the occasion of my Neighbourhood Watch party, all the residents who had accepted the Nesbitt's invitation each contributed either wine or food for the party. In my case, having had some experience of Mrs Nesbitt's *cuisine excentrique*, I decided to play for safety and had a *salade au jambon* before leaving my apartment. My contribution was three bottles of a rather good *Bordeaux Rouge*, two of which I placed on the centre table which was already packed with a wide variety of uncooked food waiting to be semi-incinerated on Malcolm's barbecue. The other bottle I opened myself, ignoring the already-opened reds and whites which, from their labels, I would classify more as battery acid than *vins des tables*. As I knew both the Nesbitts were avowed vegetarians, if not vegans, I wondered what dishes Mrs Nesbitt had prepared for herself. I was soon to find out.

'Another one of Ma Nesbitt's culinary triumphs,' said a voice behind me, as I peered towards a plate of strange, soon-to-be-cremated, greasy-grey discs, sitting limply on a bed of lettuce: 'Sage, soya, nut and chutney hamburgers. At least, that's what Malcolm said they were.'

I turned to see the testy Mr Phipps, a bottle of beer in hand, looking critically towards the various dishes and obviously trying to ascertain which ones to avoid. He pointed towards another dish, on which was piled a number of equally strange, equally unappetising, sausage-shaped objects and said:

'And those things that look like dog turds. They're supposed to be vegetarian hot-dogs. I don't know how she thinks them up,' he continued, nodding towards the seated Mrs Nesbitt, a blanket, as usual, thankfully obscuring her legs as well as supporting a baleful Alice, in her lap: 'God knows how she survives eating that sort of muck. Can't be doing her legs much good.'

I was glad I'd eaten earlier. The re-occurring vision of Mrs Nesbitt's weeping limbs was enough to kill any thoughts of further sustenance in any shape or form and I drank deeply from my glass in an attempt to blunt the unwelcome image.

There was a sudden woosh of flame from the direction of the barbecue and a strangled cry from Malcolm Nesbitt as he jumped back and slapped at his smouldering necktie, which had obviously been dangling over the barbecue that he'd finally managed to ignite. Why he had decided to wear a tie and a paisley pullover on such a sunny day was anyone's guess. Once again, Mr Phipps seemed to read my thoughts:

'The man's an idiot.'

He was about to elaborate on our host's shortcomings when Mrs Betty Ballard, from the first floor front, moved in between us and said, accusingly:

'I hear your window-cleaner has gone to prison. I read about it in the local rag.'

'Local rag?'

'Local newspaper.'

'Ah. That is correct, madame.'

'And a good thing, too. The way he preyed on all those lonely women.'

'I rather think it was the other way round.'

For a moment, she looked quite disconcerted: 'What d'you mean by that?'

I rarely comment on other people's frailties. For someone like myself, "but for the grace of God" is a phrase that comes all too readily to mind, but I was beginning to tire of the aptly-christened unmerry widow's continued high moral rectitude about everything and everyone in and around the immediate vicinity. I looked into my wine glass and said, casually:

'It seems he was more the preyed-upon than the predator. After all, none of the women involved made a complaint about him.' I then looked directly at her, played what I believe is called a hunch and said: 'And had he not been the subject of an anonymous letter to the local police, he would still be free to clean my windows.'

She flushed, slightly, then snapped: 'Even so, we still

don't want people like that frequenting Arcadia Court.'

'Oh I don't know, madame,' I said: 'I'm sure some of the residents would welcome him with open arms. In a manner of speaking.'

She flushed again, then said: 'I don't know what you are implying, Mr LaPoste, but whatever your window-cleaner may have told you - '

'I'm implying nothing, Mrs Ballard. I'm just sad that I've lost a very good window-cleaner.' I smiled brightly: 'Now, may I get you a glass of wine?'

A cold: 'No, thank you. I'll get my own.'

And she marched primly towards the centre table, her back rigid with anger. Mr Phipps, who had been listening to the exchange with increasing interest, said:

'What was all that about?'

'Can't you guess?'

He pondered for a moment and nodded, thoughtfully:

'Yes. Yes I can.' He gave one of his rare chuckles: 'I've always had my suspicions about her. Well, well, well. Now there's a thing.'

He drained his beer and went off for another bottle, shaking his head in amused disbelief. For a moment, I wondered if Mr Phipps planned to make use of the unexpected revelations concerning the secret inner urges of one of his fellow residents. But only for a moment. A widower he might be - but a masochist he wasn't.

I was about to replenish my wine glass, when two familiar voices called to me from across the garden:

'Over here, Pierre,' called Daphne.

'There's someone we'd like you to meet,' sang Deirdre.

I turned to see my favourite ex *danseuses exotiques* sitting at one of the smaller tables waving in my direction. There was a third person sitting at the table, her back towards me. I wondered what - or rather who - my friendly procurers had come up with this time and after refilling my glass, I joined the trio at their table.

'Pierre,' said Daphne: 'This is our new neighbour. She's just moved into number 27 - old Mr. Messiter's place.'

'Jenny, this is Pierre LaPoste,' said Deirdre: 'He's French.'

The woman turned in her chair to face me. Her voice was soft and musical. And in immaculate French, she said:

'Geneviève Tomlinson, Monsieur LaPoste. Enchantée.'

I was equally enchanted. The woman was remarkably attractive and for the first time since I had arrived in Muswell Hill, I was totally at a loss for words.

⋘⋙

'You fancy her, don't you, Pierre?' said Daphne archly.

'Course he does,' said Deirdre: 'It was written all over his face.'

'You looked so sweet,' said Daphne maternally: 'Like a tongue-tied teenager.'

'She fancied you, too,' said Deirdre: 'I could tell.'

'D'you really think so?' I asked eagerly, like an enamoured schoolboy at the first sight of a particularly *belle jeune fille*, across a crowded classroom.

'I know so,' said Deirdre, positively: 'After all, I am a woman.'

We were sitting around their living room table, a bottle of brandy in front of us, the barbecue having finished some time ago. I had volunteered to carry the table and chairs they'd lent for the occasion back to their apartment and had accepted their offer of a large *cognac*. I needed it. As Daphne had said, from the moment I had set eyes on the newest resident, I had acted like a *gauche* adolescent with all the hormonal problems of galloping puberty. All that was missing was the acne. In short, there had been an immediate chemical reaction from the moment I had set eyes on the delectable Geneviève Tomlinson of number 27, Arcadia Court.

On my part, at least.

It was a strange feeling. A sense of euphoria mixed with trepidation. I've always believed that the condition known as "love at first sight" was the invention of the romantic novelist and affected only those deeply into self-deception or, at best, was a form of temporary insanity that disappeared shortly after the honeymoon. After all, it is a well-known fact that the cure for love is marriage.

Now I was not so sure. Though it was certainly true in the case of my own marriage - (the cracks in our relationship started to show during our honeymoon, when she suddenly decided that too much sex caused cellulite) - it seemed very strange that seconds after meeting Geneviève Tomlinson, my first thought was to contact my wife and inform her that I was willing to give her a divorce - and the sooner the better. Now why, I wondered, should I suddenly wish to do that? It didn't make sense. Indeed, very little made sense that afternoon in July.

What did make sense was the fact that Geneviève Tomlinson's part-French, part-English name and her mastery of both the English and French languages was simply because she was the offspring of a French mother and an English father. Which also explained why, by profession, she was a translator of French-into-English and English-into-French literature, as well as acting as an interpreter at very high political and industrial levels.

She didn't stay long at the barbecue. She had, she said, to attend an official function in Whitehall later that evening, during which she would act as interpreter to a senior member of the British Foreign Office, who wished to convey to the ambassador of a third world, French-speaking country, that as far as further financial aid was concerned, they must first make use of the few millions previously given to assist their economy, but which, perhaps predictably, had ended up in their President's private Swiss bank account. It seemed that their Head of State favoured a somewhat hedonistic life-style, with a fleet of *Mercedes-Benz*, an ocean-going yacht, apartments in London, Paris and New York and had long provided a steady income for many superior *belles de nuit*.

After Miss Tomlinson had left to prepare herself for the official reception, I felt quite light-headed. Daphne nodded sagely and turned to Deirdre:

'Oh yes,' she said: 'Our Pierre's struck all right. And who wouldn't be?' she added with just a hint of envy: 'She's a very good-looking young woman.'

'Isn't she just?' agreed Deirdre, who was equally envious: 'Great legs, nice boobs, ash-blond hair that didn't come out of a bottle, lovely green eyes and sexy with it. Looks like Betty Grable on a good day.'

'Betty Grable?'

Deirdre looked at me and smiled her maternal smile: 'Before your time, darling.'

Said Daphne: 'And unless I'm mistaken, that dress she was wearing was a *Givenchy*.'

They were silent for a moment, then Daphne took a sip of brandy and said:

'It's not fair, is it?'

'No,' said Deirdre: 'It bloody isn't. Why did the cow have to turn up here?'

'Now really!' I protested, remembering the meaningless phrase that the English invariably use to express outrage: 'Now really!' I repeated, recalling an equally meaningless English expression: 'You're really out of order, there.'

'Just teasing, Pierre,' said Deirdre: 'We liked her the moment we saw her. We met in the lift.'

'How old d'you think she is?' asked Daphne.

Deirdre considered: 'Oh, at a guess, in her thirties. Say thirty-two or three.'

'A couple of years younger than me,' I said, unaccountably pleased with her surmise. Then I thought for a moment and said, aloud: 'Now why did I say that?'

'We've told you,' said Daphne: 'Because you've got the hots for her.'

'Pity she's married,' sighed Deirdre: 'Or I reckon you'd have been well way there.'

'She's married?'

They both nodded, sadly and all the euphoria generated at my first sight of the delectable Geneviève Tomlinson evaporated in an instant, to be replaced with a cloud of gloom that hovered overhead like the pall of smoke from the massed barbecues of Muswell Hill.

My disappointment was obvious: 'You're saying it's *Mrs* Tomlinson?'

'That's what she told us,' said Daphne: 'Seems she's married to an Englishman.'

Why, I thought, despondently, had I assumed otherwise? A woman as attractive as she? Of course she was married. She had to be.

'Poor Pierre,' said Daphne, sympathetically: 'We finally

introduce you to some one you could go for and she's already spoken for.'

I didn't sleep very well that evening. In fact, I didn't sleep very well for the next few days. The morning after the barbecue, I woke up feeling exceedingly nauseous and after rummaging through my briefcase, I found the signed and stamped E111 form which covered medical care while in another member country of the European Union and decided to make use of it. In between throwing-up, I showered, got dressed and set out for the nearest doctor's surgery. Which was the most sensible thing I had done in the last 24 hours.

◈

Doctor Patel was most unlike my general medical practitioner back in Ménerbes. Of Asian descent, she was short, rotund, wore an immaculate white coat and a permanent smile. As she took my temperature and blood pressure, I couldn't help comparing her approach with that of her Ménerbes equivalent who, with a *Disque Bleu* dangling from the corner of his mouth, would wheezingly inform me that all I needed was a stiff shot of *anisette* to cure me of any ailment I thought I might have.

Doctor Patel checked the readings and said, positively:

'You've obviously eaten something that has disagreed with you.'

Well, well, well, I thought, sourly. All those years of training and that's the best you can come up with? To my shame, I have to confess that, like most men, be they French or English, whenever I feel off-colour, I resent all those around me who are not sharing the same pain and discomfort.

'Are you sure that's all it is?' I said: 'I feel terrible.'

'Well yes, you would,' said the good doctor: 'Food poisoning is very debilitating. A lot of people die from it,' she added cheerfully: 'Can you remember what you've had to eat during the last 24 hours?'

'Not a lot. Just a ham salad and a - '

I paused as I remembered, with increasing alarm that, while engrossed in a starry-eyed conversation with the lovely Geneviève Tomlinson, I had absently nibbled on one of Malcolm Nesbitt's semi-scorched vegetarian hot-dogs. It had tasted foul but I had been too absorbed to care.

'You need to go for a blood test,' said the doctor, scribbling on a green form and handing it to me: 'The Whittington hospital on Highgate Hill. Take the 134 bus to Archway. In the meantime,' she continued, tapping out a prescription on her computer: 'Drop this in at the chemists - it should help with your incontinence.'

'But I'm not incontinent,' I pointed out.

'You will be,' she said, prophetically, handing me the prescription: 'Especially if you don't take this medication.'

I thanked her politely, threw-up once again in the surgery toilet, dropped the prescription into a drug-store on the Broadway called *Boots* - (which I'd previously assumed was a footwear emporium) - and took the 134 to Archway without further mishap, if only because there was nothing left to throw up.

The Whittington hospital proved to be a collection of large, rambling Victorian buildings on both sides of Highgate Hill, some modernised and others in the process of being modernised. These included, I later discovered, a sombre, grey-brick edifice that had once been a workhouse - that final refuge for the local poor, sick and destitute, so vividly described by the English writer Charles Dickens in his novel *Oliver Twist*.

I wondered if it was by accident or design that the old workhouse conveniently overlooked Highgate cemetery, a well-known last resting place for the Victorian rich, famous and notorious. Its residents include operatic impresario Sir Richard D'Oyly Carte, the novelist Mary Ann Evans who, for reasons probably best known to herself, wrote under the pseudonym of George Elliot, the itinerant revolutionary Karl Marx and numerous victims of the Great Plague, still hermetically sealed in a common tomb beneath St. Michael's Church.

Feeling extremely mortal, I wondered if I was destined to join those same dear departed, just over the wall from the hospital. As the doctor had pointed out, food poisoning could prove fatal and even though Malcolm Nesbitt, in all seriousness, had once informed me that death was just nature's way of telling us to slow down, it was with great foreboding that I took the escalator to the blood-test clinic, on the fourth level of the diagnostic block.

The Whittington hospital, I was later told, is one of the busiest in London and on that Monday morning, it was living up to its reputation. The waiting room was packed with patients waiting their turn to have their veins punctured by the resident Count Draculas, as the Seymour nursing twins had once amusingly described them. But despite this, within the hour I had reached the head of the queue and was promptly and painlessly relieved of three small phials of blood. It was when I was walking towards the down escalator for transportation to the ground floor that I heard a familiar voice:

'Hallo, sunshine,' said the pretty nurse as she came up behind me.

'What are you doing here?' said her identical twin.

Passing male patients looked openly envious as the Seymour sisters planted a kiss on each cheek.

'We were going to ask you to come to a party at our place but we didn't have your phone number,' said Cindy.

'First Saturday in August, seven-thirty,' said Angie: 'Can you make it?'

'If I'm still alive,' I said, looking suitably pathetic: 'I've been food-poisoned.'

'You'll be all right,' said Angie with professional confidence.

'If not,' said Cindy: 'Just tell the undertaker to let us know when the funeral is.'

Another sisterly kiss on the cheek and they were gone. By the time I reached the main entrance, the prospect of seeing the twins again made me feel a little better. In their own way, they were just as desirable as the fragrant Geneviève Tomlinson and while I realised that the chances of bringing any relationship with either or both of them to a carnal conclusion were extremely remote, it would help to take my mind off the unattainable Geneviève.

I came out of the *No Smoking* hospital and made my way across the carpet of cigarette ends on the pavement, weaving through the numerous patients standing around the doorway, all puffing desperately on their cigarettes, before they finally went back inside, presumably to be given a chest X-ray, followed by a few hours on an iron lung.

∽∾

Returning to Muswell Hill, I collected my prescription from the chemists and took a large swig of the foul-tasting concoction, which I assumed was designed to plug certain orifices to create an effect similar to that of an egg-bound chicken. It appeared to work - for the moment, at least - and I prepared to spend the rest of the day in bed. It was late evening when I was awakened by the persistent and non-stop ringing of my doorbell. Moving groggily towards the door, dressed in only my Y-fronts, I called through the letterbox:

'Who is it?'

'*C'est moi, chéri!*' came the reply: '*Ouvre la porte!*'

I shook my head in disbelief. Surely not. It couldn't be. But it was. The moment I opened the door, the plumply-pretty Michelle from the *Pâtisserie de Ménerbes*, dropped her suitcase, hurled herself into my arms and buried her head against my chest, the tears streaming down her cheeks:

'*Oh Pierre! Mon amour! Tu m'as tellement manqué!*'

'Oh *merde*,' I thought, for more reasons than one, as I was suddenly forced to disentangle myself and run for the toilet. When I emerged, some time later, I found the now even plumper Michelle curled up in my bed, sound asleep. She had obviously had a long and arduous journey. For a moment, despite my *mal d'estomac*, I contemplated joining her. After all, old habits die hard. But I decided against it. Michelle was obviously in Muswell Hill for a purpose and I first had to find out just what that purpose was.

AUGUST

T HE FIRST SATURDAY IN AUGUST was fast approaching and I had still not left for Ménerbes. I had planned to leave at the end of the previous month and be back in good time for the Seymour sisters' party, but on account of my unwanted guest, I was still tied to Muswell Hill. The night she arrived, I had slept in the guest room, to be awakened the following morning by a smiling Michelle with a cup of *café* and a bright:

'*Bonjour, chéri. Ça va?*'

'Feeling much better, thank you,' I said automatically, in English. It would seem I had been Anglified without even being aware of it: '*Pardon, Michelle,*' I continued quickly: '*Ça va bien, merci. Et vous?*'

'*Toi,*' she said reprovingly, then sitting on the end of my bed, she had poured out her woes in graphic detail, occasionally punctuating her narrative with a sniff, a tear or a bitter expletive.

It appeared that, as I had anticipated, amorous undertaker Gaston Lafarge had scuttled around to the back door of the *pâtisserie* the moment he heard I was bound for foreign parts. In my absence and at a loose end, it hadn't taken Michelle long to succumb to the blandishments of the smooth-talking funeral director and, after a time, she had become attached to him. At fairly regular intervals, as it were.

Knowing I was still married and unlikely to seek my freedom in the foreseeable future, she had pragmatically shifted her matrimonial sights on to the still vigorous Monsieur Lafarge, with his own business and a comfortable *maison* in Ménerbes. But just a few days ago, she had walked unexpectedly into his establishment, to find her designated husband in the act of energetically comforting the rich and quite voluptuous widow of a recently deceased client, on top of the laying-out table, in the chapel of rest.

'I didn't know what to do, Pierre. I trusted him, you see, even though he had taken advantage of me within hours of you leaving for England. But I knew I had to do something.' She dabbed at her eyes and said, pathetically: 'Then I thought of you. *Mon ami et mon amour.* So I got your address from *Le Courrier* - '

'How did you manage that? They had no right to disclose - '

'Oh, it was easy. I just told them I was your *fiancée* who'd just found out she was pregnant.'

'Pregnant? You actually told them that?'

'Yes.'

'And are you pregnant?'

She examined her finger nails and gave an almost imperceptible nod:

'Un peu.'

'A bit? What does that mean?'

'It isn't due for months, yet.'

'How many months?'

'Seven. Or maybe eight.'

I gave an inward sigh of relief. After all, Michelle and I

had once been embroiled in a long and exceedingly lively relationship and it was comforting to know that the additional *kilos* she had acquired since the last time I'd seen her, were seemingly due to her continuing *penchant* for cream pastries, rather than any of our past extra-curricular activities.

'Congratulations,' I said, from the heart: 'To both of you.'

'I haven't told him yet. That's why I've got to do something, before the old bastard moves in with Madame Bécus, just because of her money.'

'Even so, I really don't see what I can do.'

'I don't want you to do anything. Just let me stay here a while - until he finds out how much he misses me and begs me to come back to Ménerbes. As I'm sure he will,' she went on, earnestly: 'You've no idea how jealous he is of any man with whom I once had an *histoire de coeur* - you in particular. He's never liked you. Ever since he found out what a great lover you were.'

'How could he possibly know that?''

'Because I told him. Every time we made love. Made him furious - I can't think why - and when he finds out I'm here, he'll go *ballistique*.'

'But how will he find out?'

'I left a note on his desk, with your address and telephone number.'

Even for Michelle, who had never been over-burdened with intelligence, her optimism about both the reactions or intentions of Monsieur Lafarge was obviously somewhat misplaced. But I could hardly refuse to take part in the *charade*, if only for old time's sake.

'Very well,' I said reluctantly: 'You can stay. For just a few days, mind. To give Lafarge time to find out what he's missing and call you.'

And *cochons* might fly, I thought sadly, to myself. Then seeing her doleful demeanour, I added a reassuring:

'He'll soon realise how lucky he is to have a girl like you.'

Michelle beamed, then nodded, positively: 'And so he should. I've been loyal, loving and completely faithful from the moment we first met.' She stood up and began to unbutton her blouse: 'Now finish your coffee and we'll go to bed.'

In the event, I pleaded the traditional excuse of a debilitating headache and decided, there and then, to remain in the guest room until it was time for her to depart. Should Monsieur Lafarge fail to contact her, which was a strong possibility, I had no wish to give Michelle even the smallest excuse for demanding to stay on indefinitely, because of a re-kindled relationship. Several days and no telephone calls later, I decided the time had come for her to leave for Ménerbes - if only because it was quite impossible for me to write my column while she sat all day and most of the evening, in front of a blaring television set, dressed only in a revealing baby-doll night-dress, the telephone by her side, my biscuit-barrel in her lap, munching away steadily, while trying to understand the plots of the interminable English and Australian television soap operas, without the benefit of French subtitles.

Too frightened to leave the telephone unattended, the only time she ventured out of the apartment was to make a quick foray into the Broadway, to stock up on cakes, pastries and biscuits to sustain her during her ordeal. While she spoke little or no English, she managed to communicate with the local bakery assistants by sign language, grunts and miming the act of mastication. At first, until they realised she was French and therefore, like all foreigners, a trifle touched in the *tête*, her performance must have been quite unnerving.

My subtle hints that she was over-staying her welcome were met with blank, wide-eyed incomprehension and short of packing her suitcase while she was out on one of her cake-buying expeditions, then leaving it outside my front door, there seemed to be little else I could do to get the message across. The girl had elevated obtuseness to a fine art and I came to the reluctant conclusion that in order to secure the peace and tranquillity I needed to do my job, I had no option but to again seek refuge at Mrs Kwiatkowska's *Savoy Private Guest House*. At least, I wouldn't have far to walk to attend the Seymour sisters' party.

That morning, after sleeping late, Michelle had padded into the living room, attired, as usual, in her baby-doll night-dress and when I informed her (quite untruthfully) that I had to go out of town for a few days on business, she did not take kindly to the thought she would be left entirely on her own in a strange town, in a strange country. It appeared that this was the first occasion she'd actually travelled further than Aix-en-Provence in her entire life, but when I told her I would arrange for a daily delivery of assorted pastries from the local *pâtisserie*, she grudgingly wished me *bon voyage*, reached for the biscuit barrel and switched on the television.

Because of my reluctance to resume where we'd left off, all those months ago, which she was more than willing to do - if only because it would alleviate the tedium of waiting for her lover to telephone - she had, by now, given-up on me and didn't really care if I was around or not. I packed a suitcase, unplugged my laptop and set off in the direction of *The Savoy*, via the bakery, to arrange for Michelle's daily supply of sustenance.

❧

It was only a couple of days after I'd settled into my original bed-sitter that I remembered that actor-cleaner Maggie Turnbull was due to pay me a visit the following day and I reached for the telephone to inform the non-English-speaking Michelle who Maggie was, why she was there and to allow her into the apartment.

The phone rang and rang. There was no reply and I hazarded a guess that she had decided to slip out to the *pâtisserie* to make her own choice of cream-cakes, rather than simply accept what was being delivered to her. I rang an hour later. There was still no reply and I was beginning to feel quite concerned. Where on earth could she have got to?

There was only one thing to do. I closed down my computer and walked briskly up the hill towards *Arcadia Court*. I ran up the steps to the front doors and was moving towards the elevator when the lift-doors opened and Deirdre and Daphne emerged.

'Ah, Pierre!' said Daphne: 'Just the man we want to see.'

'We have something to tell you,' said Deirdre.

'We certainly have,' said Daphne.

Despite the urgency of my need to find out why Michelle had failed to answer the telephone, I had no wish to offend my two favourite neighbours and told myself that a few minutes more wouldn't make any difference.

Said Deirdre, with a wicked gleam in her eye: 'D'you want the good news first or the really good news?'

'Er... the good news, please.'

'Geneviève Tomlinson has invited us to dinner and asked us the number of your flat, so she can invite you, too.'

Said Daphne archly: 'She said you were very charming to her at the barbecue and she'd found you *tray genteel* - whatever that means.'

'Doesn't it mean he's not Jewish?' asked Deirdre.

I smiled: 'No, it doesn't. She must have said *gentil*, not gen*tile*. Which means in French... well, nice and kind.'

'Hear that?' said Deirdre, to Daphne: 'Seems Pierre's cracked it.'

I should have felt pleased, but I wasn't. What would be the point? The last thing I wished to do was meet her husband, for whom I had already acquired a deep and all-consuming loathing. To have acquired a wife of such splendour, Tomlinson obviously had to be as handsome as an Adonis, with all the legendary wit and charm of an Oxford-educated, upper-class Englishman - if that is what he was. If he wasn't, he should have been. My lack of enthusiasm to dine with the Tomlinsons was obvious.

'Oh,' I said: 'How very kind of them. But I'm afraid I'm pretty tied up for the next few weeks.'

Said Daphne, with an equally wicked gleam in her eye: 'When you hear the really good news, I think you may wish to untie yourself.'

'And what's that?'

'She's not married,' said Deirdre: 'So how does that grab you?'

'Well, when we say she's not married,' said Daphne: 'Though she's still Mrs Tomlinson, it seems she's in the process of getting a divorce. That's why she moved into *Arcadia Court*.'

My delight was palpable.

'Oh,' I said again: 'In that case, I do seem to have a few evenings free.'

Les Girls giggled: 'Surprise, surprise.'

'Did she actually mention a date?' I asked.

'No. She said she'd drop round to your flat and have a word with you.'

Why, I wondered, did I have a sudden sense of deep foreboding? A moment later, I knew very well why and eschewing the creaking lift, I shouted an apology at the startled Deirdre and Daphne and raced for the stairs, climbing them three at a time.

When I opened the door, I found, as I had half expected, that Michelle had packed her suitcase and departed. The long, rambling note on the dining room table said it all. While, thankfully, Michelle was no longer part of my life, after what she had apparently said to the French-speaking lady to whom she'd opened the door, it was extremely doubtful if Geneviève Tomlinson would ever be part of it, either.

I deciphered Michelle's mostly mis-spelt, childish scrawl with some difficulty. Although she had not bothered to add a single *aigu* or *grave accent, cédille* or *circonflexe* to her message, in the best traditions of the semi-literate, she had generously sprinkled it with a plethora of misplaced *apostrophes*, with a blithe disregard for French grammar.

Mon amour, she had written: *Merci beaucoup pour votre hospitalite, vo's gateau'x a la crem'e et les biscuit's au chocolat's, mais je retourn a Menerbe's immediatment.*

In France, as in England, unnecessary apostrophes abounded throughout the nation, seemingly breeding like *lapins* on Viagra. Indeed, a noted English journalist, novelist and playwright, in a vain attempt to stem the flow of the gratuitous apostrophe, had founded the aptly-named AAAA - *The Association for the Abolition of the Aberrant Apostrophe* - and appointed himself Life President. But that proved to be of little help to me when trying to unravel Michelle's tortuous syntax.

Roughly translated, it seemed that she had indeed finally received a telephone call from Ménerbes - not from her *mortician manqué*, but from the aforementioned Madame Bécus, the rich widow to whom he had transferred his affections. While visiting him at his place of business, Madame Bécus had found his office to be unoccupied, but before leaving, she had happened upon the carelessly-discarded note the unhappy Michelle had left behind, before running away to England.

She had read its contents with rising anger. Previously unaware of her lover's association with an employee of the local *pâtisserie* at the same time he was courting her, she stormed into the chapel of rest only to discover the indefatigable Monsieur Lafarge in *fragrante delicto* - this time, in the process of comforting the rosy-cheeked young woman from the local *Café-Tabac*, who had, it seemed, recently split up with her gentleman-friend. Somewhat predictably, unable to resist an opportunity to help any vulnerable *jeune fille* in her hour of need, he was unselfishly offering consolation in the only way he knew - and with obvious enthusiasm.

On reading that part of the note, I had a sudden feeling of amused *déjà-vu* and wondered if Monsieur Lafarge, before becoming an undertaker, had first started out as a window-cleaner and had, like the now incarcerated Freddie Finnegan, succumbed to the demands of the profession and acquired a taste for serial philandering. After all, one had to start somewhere.

I returned to the letter to discover that the same Madame Bécus had, very kindly, telephoned Michelle in London, informed her that as she and their joint ex-lover were no longer what the English call "an item," there was now no reason for her to remain in London. It was when Michelle sobbingly informed her of her condition that a shocked Madame Bécus had told her to fear not and to return home immediately.

On her return, the widow proposed that the two of them, plus the equally outraged woman from the *Café-Tabac* (who had also been under the impression that she was the undertaker's one and only *amoureuse*) would confront the multiple-seducer face-to-face on the steps of the local *église*, in the presence of the priest and demand that he make an honest woman of the mother of his child-to-be. Otherwise, she had added grimly, they would publicly shame him in front of the entire congregation.

In a small village like Ménerbes, no one survives that sort of *exposé publique*, either socially or commercially. And from the letter and wedding photograph I received from Michelle a few weeks later, it seemed that Madame Bécus' strategy had worked and Gaston Lafarge had wisely, if reluctantly, taken the only option left open to him. Knowing Michelle would watch over her new husband, day and night, with the ferocity of a female rattlesnake protecting her habitat, ready and willing to bury her fangs into any other female who had the temerity to waggle her rattle invitingly in the direction of her husband, it would seem that Gaston Lafarge's days as the *Casanova de Ménerbes* were over.

At least, with Michelle no longer a threat to my freedom, there was now no need to deny my wife a divorce and I resolved to write and tell her so, providing it was on the grounds of her quite shameless adultery and that her plastic surgeon lover would pay all the costs involved. After all, he obviously had a great deal more money than I had and even if it turned out be extremely costly, all he'd have to do is whip out his scalpel and enhance a few more mammary glands, lift an extra face or two, or nip-and-tuck the odd drooping *derrière*.

At the same time, while Michelle's predicament had obviously been brought to a relatively satisfactory conclusion, my own had been exacerbated by her mere presence in my apartment. My world had fallen apart the day she had opened the door to Geneviève Tomlinson. Unfortunately, Michelle had been dressed, as usual, in her skimpy baby-doll nightdress, which to anyone but her, would have implied a certain intimacy between host and house-guest. But the sting was in the last paragraph of her note:

I don't know why, but the woman seemed to be a bit taken-aback that I was there and asked if I was your wife. When I told her I wasn't - just a girlfriend and that your real wife lived in Paris, she looked quite surprised. When I asked her if she wanted to leave a message, she said no. Not now. She apologised for disturbing me and left. I've no idea what she wanted, but I thought you'd like to know she called.

The telephone rang just as I finished reading Michelle's note.

'What have you been up to, you naughty boy?' said Daphne over the phone: 'Geneviève has just rung up to say you won't be coming to dinner as you're obviously otherwise engaged. She seemed a little upset. You're not otherwise engaged, are you?'

'As far as she's concerned, I am. And not only engaged,

but living with a fat little French girl, even though I've got a wife who lives in Paris.'

'And have you?' asked Deirdre, on the extension.

'Sort of, yes.'

'Dam' fool,' said Daphne: 'How did you get yourself into such a mess?'

'It's a long story,' I said wearily: 'Now if you'll excuse me, I have to write my last-will-and-testament and a suicide note.'

In the event, I put down the phone and reached for a bottle of whiskey, instead.

❧

I did not go to the Seymour sisters' party. I was far too depressed and had no wish to join any social gathering with a face that would curdle *le lait*. Neither did I attempt to contact Madame Tomlinson to explain that I was not in a relationship with the cheerfully uninhibited Michelle, or indeed, with anyone else for that matter and that while I did have a wife living in Paris, she had abandoned me for some one else.

Sadly, I had come to the conclusion that the circumstantial evidence was far too strong for me to have any hope of being believed. To be honest, I would have had great difficulty in believing it myself and I was resigned to ending a potentially beautiful friendship before it had even begun.

The best therapy, I reasoned, would be to bury my sorrows under a greater workload and I telephoned my travel editor in Paris. He immediately agreed that, for the benefit of *Le Courrier's* readers intent on touring the English provinces, I should sample a number of country hotels and restaurants as far afield as Wales in the West, Norfolk in the East, Sussex in the South and both sides of the Pennines, in the North.

I decided to first travel North, where I intended to search out the better hotels and restaurants that undoubtedly existed in the Yorkshire and Lancashire wastelands, but with which few *touristes Français* were familiar.

Accordingly, I took the *Métro* to London's King's Cross railway terminus where, in my efforts to purchase a ticket to the largest city in Yorkshire, I was confronted with a bewildering series of options as to how, where and when I would travel. Such was the complexity of the available options, I cannot recall those options in detail. Moreover, my confusion was intensified by a verbal exchange with the pleasant, but somewhat under-enthusiastic lady booking clerk. Though our conversation started off quite normally, it quickly metamorphosed, as usual, into the bizarre:

'A ticket to Leeds, please.'

'At what time d'you wish to travel, sir?' asked the clerk, reluctantly punching up some figures on her computer.

'As soon as possible.'

'Today?'

'Of course.'

A shake of the head: 'Not a good idea, sir. After all, it is Wednesday. And four minutes past eleven hundred hours.'

'So?'

'In the interests of good customer relations, I am required to inform you that during the period of eleven hundred hours to fourteen forty-two hours, the second-class fare to Leeds, one way, has a twenty-five percent surcharge.'

'Why?'

A sigh and sad shake of the head:

'I've no idea why, sir. I just tell you what they've told me to tell you and our latest tariffs are as follows.' She took a deep breath, then at lighting speed and as if by rote, she launched into a flood of statistics that (as perhaps was intended) left me totally baffled.

'If you intend to travel first class outside the allotted times, the surcharge rises to thirty-seven percent - but only on Tuesdays. On a Wednesday, there is an across-the-board surcharge of forty-two percent, so it is in your interests to delay your journey until a later or earlier date - like Monday or Thursday - but not Saturday, of course, which carries a weekend penalty of seventy-two per-cent between nine-hundred and eleven-hundred hours.'

'Seventy-two per-cent?'

She nodded, cheerfully: 'Outrageous, isn't it?'

Then looking left and right over her shoulder, she lowered her voice, leaned closer towards the communications window and said:

'I shouldn't be telling you this sir, but we do it to discourage the soccer hooligans from travelling with us for away matches.'

From where I was standing, their ticket-sales policy seemed to be designed to discourage anyone from travelling anywhere. Perhaps their accountants had done a few sums and come to the conclusion that the more customers they could confuse and alienate, the fewer the number of trains they would have to provide which, in turn, would mean less wear-and-tear on the station concourse, fewer repairs to the track and enable a sizeable reduction in the work force.

'So what's it to be, sir?' she said, with an obvious lack of interest, seemingly keen to switch off her computer and take a coffee-break.

'A first-class return ticket to Leeds.'

'For when, sir?

'Today.'

She looked quite disappointed: 'Are you sure, sir? If you booked seven days in advance, the cost would be substantially less. And if you booked twenty-eight days in advance, the cost would be halved.'

I couldn't help wondering what would happen if I booked a year in advance. Would the railway company pay *me*?

Again I said: 'I wish to travel today.'

After all, I wouldn't be paying for it.

A deep sigh: 'Very well, sir. At what time do you wish to travel?'

'Right now.'

An even deeper sigh: 'As you wish, sir.'

Her inability to persuade me (in my own best interests, of course) to postpone my journey or even not travel at all was obviously, to her at least, an admission of failure and would not go down well with her superiors. It was with a look of deep reproach that she printed out my ticket, charged my credit card and directed me to the platform for Leeds which, my guidebook had informed me, was once the centre of the English woollen industry and a good starting point for my culinary expedition into the provinces.

The train departed on time and I settled down in my seat to enjoy the journey which, despite the relatively Spartan comfort and *décor* compared to a *Eurostar* or *TGV* compartment, it would, I thought, be interesting to view the English countryside while sipping a *café filtre*, as promised on the first-class menu. Unfortunately, the moment the train moved out of the station, most of my travelling companions in the fairly crowded carriage, whipped out their mobile telephones and, as one, dialled a number, before all loudly chorusing:

'I'm on the train.'

This, I gather, has now become an English ritual that is repeated on all forms of transport across the nation. The large, bluff man with a florid complexion and a well-cut business suit sitting opposite me replaced his telephone, opened his briefcase, took out a wad of papers and spread them across the table. In a strong Northern accent he said:

'Don't mind, do you? Got to finish these before we get to Wakefield.'

'Not at all.'

He looked at me with interest: 'You're not from round here, are you?'

'I'm French.'

He nodded, sagely: 'Thought you weren't from my part of the world. What are you doing over here?'

I told him.

'Starting off in Leeds, eh? You're in for a treat. We've got the best fish-and-chip shops in the North. Not like the muck they serve up in the South.'

It appeared that the traditional dish of fish-and-chips was beloved by all Northerners, irrespective of income or social class, having apparently been their main source of nourishment since birth. Possibly even before being weaned. My travelling companion warmed to his theme:

'They say there are some good chip shops down South, but I've never come across one. And d'you know why they're no dam' good? I'll tell you why.' He leaned forward across the table and, in tones of total incredulity, said: 'You're not going to believe this, but instead of skinning the fish before they cook it - like they do in the North - the Southerners serve their battered cod with the skins left on!' He shook his head in total disbelief: 'Can you imagine that? Gross, isn't it? If any Northern chippy tried to get away with doing that, their only clientele would be the bloody bailiffs.'

As I'd never actually eaten either Northern or Southern English fish-and-chips, all I could do was shake my own head, as if in sympathy with the horror of it all.

'And I'll tell you something else you might find hard to believe - they actually fry their fish in cooking-oil. Yes, cooking-oil. Not in the traditional beef dripping which, as everyone knows, not only adds flavour to the chips, but fries at a much higher temperature - which is why, of course, the batter always comes out crisp and crunchy.'

He was almost salivating at the thought.

'But will the Southerners listen? Will they buggery. They just go on about how unhealthy beef dripping is. But what else can you expect from a bunch of wishy-washy, namby-pamby, arty-farty, poofty-woofty Southerners?'

I'd heard of the so-called North-South divide and, listening to him, it was obviously alive and well and living in Wakefield:

'Unhealthy?' he repeated, his face turning puce at the thought: 'Beef dripping has been the making of Yorkshire. We've been eating it for generations and it hasn't done us any harm. I mean, look at me.'

I looked at him, crimson-complexioned and wide of girth and wondered if he'd manage to reach Wakefield without me being obliged to give him mouth-to-mouth resuscitation in the event of a heart attack - the prospect of which had little appeal. Even so, it was because of his gratuitous lecture on the merits of Northern fish-and-chip shops that I decided to delay my investigation into the hotels and restaurants of the North and, while in Leeds, try to discover what all the fuss was about. Even if my cholesterol levels went temporarily into overdrive, it would make an interesting little piece for *Le Courrier*.

It was not an unpleasant journey, despite the number of times the train came to a halt due to a wide variety of unfortunate set-backs, involving leaves on the line, no leaves on the line, repairs to the track, no repairs to the track and the need to stop at Doncaster to re-stock the buffet-car that, much to the embarrassment of the buffet-car attendant, had run out of the other vital part of every Northerner's daily diet: a circular, muffin-shaped piece of buttered bread - or bap - in which was sandwiched a piece of fried bacon and, according to my travelling companion, was called a "bacon-butty."

He further informed me, perhaps slightly *langue*-in-cheek, that in the same way every true Scotsman is obliged to carry an oat cake in his sporran, a true Northerner is very rarely without a cold bacon-butty in his trousers pocket, wrapped up in page three of the previous day's copy of *The Daily Sport* newspaper.

I said farewell to my travelling companion, who wheezed off the train at Wakefield and I finally arrived at Leeds main-line station twenty minutes late (which I was told was most unusual - the delays were normally much longer). I checked into my hotel, examined the list of several fish-and-chip establishments so kindly provided by my travelling companion and decided to make the short taxi journey out of town to the most famous chip shop of them all.

✎৯৯

"Chip Shop" turned out to be something of a misnomer. Housed in a large, red-brick building that resembled an omnibus garage, with an interior illuminated by giant chandeliers, the place was big enough to accommodate the many individual diners, coach parties and family-outings and, at the same time, cater for the long queue at the take-away counter.

I didn't have long to wait for a table and, at the recommendation of the motherly waitress, I ordered and was served with an enormous piece of battered haddock and a bowl of what were described on the menu as "mixed vegetables." The first of the three vegetables turned out to be a bright green pulp made from dried *pois*, which sits on the plate (and the stomach) like a sullen reproach for too much self-indulgence and is what the English call "mushy peas."

The second vegetable was described as "scallops," but which were merely circular discs of *pomme de terre* fried in crispy batter. The last was simply a pile of *pommes frites*. The meal was apparently not complete without a pot of English breakfast tea and a plate of "mixed" bread and butter. In other words, white bread and brown. But despite my initial misgivings, I enjoyed every mouthful.

While I shuddered to think how much that one meal had reduced my life expectancy, I was more than prepared to repeat the process during my sojourn in the North. As my travelling companion had said, beef dripping undoubtedly added an extra dimension to the dish that he claimed had been the staple diet of Northerners since the War of the Roses. I had naturally assumed that this armed confrontation had been over which side got the pick of the local cod and haddock fishing grounds, but it seemed that this was not so. He explained it had simply been a difference of opinion between the rival aristocratic houses of York and Lancaster over who should rule England after King Henry V1 had "gone quite ga-ga," as he put it, seemingly an occupational hazard of most of the inter-bred English aristocracy. Then as now, he implied. Even so, I still couldn't help wondering if the victor's spoils of war had included the other's supply of beef dripping, skinned *poissons*, scallops, chips and mushy peas.

'A chip, a chip, my Kingdom for a chip!' I had said with a smile, roguishly misquoting Shakespeare's Richard III. My travelling companion had not smiled in return. Perhaps, as in the case of Mr Phipps, it was the way I told it. But I was pleased he had introduced me to this Northern delicacy. Not that I had any intention of admitting to the readers of *Le Courrier* that I had actually enjoyed such traditional English fare. The French have always considered themselves to be *maitres de la cuisine*, who could not possibly have anything to learn from the English.

The more is the pity, for I have to admit that while practising my profession, I've had more then my fair share of "innovative" French cooking, all of which looked and tasted as unpleasant as the equally innovative Mrs Nesbitt's famed, if also inedible, anchovy-turnip-and-marmalade flans.

It took me to the end of August to complete my tour of Northern English watering places and, on my return to Muswell Hill to complete my pieces for Le Courrier, I became a virtual recluse. I had no wish to take part in any of Arcadia Court's social activities, if only to avoid the embarrassing possibility of bumping into Geneviève Tomlinson. But in a small community like ours, I knew it would only be a matter of time before I came face-to-face with my unrequited love. And because of the intervention of a certain actor-cleaner, it came sooner than I thought.

SEPTEMBER

I
T WAS COLD IN SEPTEMBER. But Malcolm
Nesbitt's cheerful greeting was warm enough: 'We
haven't seen you around for ages. Where have you
been hiding yourself?'

'I've been away. On business.'

'Ah, well, that explains it, doesn't it?' As usual, he
answered himself: 'Yes. It certainly does.'

As we were sharing *Arcadia Court's* lethargic lift to the
fourth floor, I was his captive audience for all of three
minutes, which was more than enough time for Malcolm to
bring me up to date with everything that had happened in my
absence:

'Mother saw a specialist at the Whittington who gave her
some new pills which seem to be working and her legs are
beginning to dry-out quite nicely. Alice sniffed out some
more mushrooms at the old race-course and as usual, piddled
all over them.' He chuckled at the memory: '"Naughty
Alice," I said to her: "Naughty, naughty little Alice." But she
just gave me that funny little grin of hers and you can't help
but smile, can you?'

Oh yes, I can, I thought.

'Why don't you give little Alice one of your mother's new pills?' I suggested.

He looked at me blankly: 'Why on earth should I want to do that?'

'Perhaps it would have a similar effect on little Alice's weak bladder as it's having on your mother's weeping legs.'

'Oh, I very much doubt it,' he said seriously: 'Besides, it's not Alice's fault. She just can't help herself. Never could. The moment she sees a mushroom, she has to turn on the waterworks.'

By now, I was beginning to get a trifle weary with Malcolm's preoccupation with all things urinary and I silently pleaded with the lift to get a move on and let me seek sanctuary in the privacy of my apartment. But Malcolm was just getting into his stride:

'Mr. Phipps has had his foot in plaster since last Sunday, after breaking three of his toes.'

'Bowls,' I said automatically.

'No, it's not,' insisted Malcolm: 'It really happened. When he was playing... ah, I see what you mean.'

Mr Phipps had obviously come up against the geriatric psychopath. Malcolm continued to go through his list:

'Mrs Baxter of the first floor front has had new windows put in. Seems she was cleaning the old ones and the glass fell out.'

I couldn't help smiling. I remembered what Mr Phipps had said about Old Aspidistra Face, as he insisted upon calling her - that she'd cleaned her windows so often, the glass had to be paper-thin. He'd obviously been closer to the truth than he'd realised.

Continued Malcolm: 'What else? Oh yes. The two theatrical ladies from number 37 have had their feet done.'

'Their feet done?'

'By me. I'm a visiting chiropodist. That's what I do for a living. Didn't you know?'

I didn't. But it seemed to explain a lot about Malcolm. I wasn't sure why, but somehow, in his case, in-growing toenails and paisley pullovers seemed to go together.

'Mother was very pleased when I decided to follow in my father's footsteps, as it were. He was a chiropodist, too,' he added unnecessarily: 'Oh yes, she thinks it's nice to have a chiropodist around the house. Because of those legs of hers, she's always had trouble with her feet.'

For one lunatic moment, I wondered if every time Malcolm tended his mother's troubled feet, he had to wear a shower-cap. By the time I had managed to exorcise this unwelcome image, the lift had finally ground to a halt. As we parted in the corridor, Malcolm added a coda to his potted review of events:

'And oh yes, Mrs Tomlinson who recently moved into number 27 - her who was at my barbecue - '

I froze like a pointer *chien* on a grouse shoot:

'What about her?'

'She's throwing a flat-warming party on Friday. Everyone's invited, so I'll see you there, no doubt.'

He wiggled his fingers in farewell and walked off down the corridor. See me there? I didn't think so. I opened the door of my apartment, walked in and tripped over the pile of junk mail and letters that had accumulated during my trip to the North. As I expected, an invitation to Geneviève Tomlinson's flat-warming party was not amongst them. One letter, with a Paris postmark, stood out from all the others. It was from my wife, in which she coldly thanked me for agreeing to a divorce, adding that she had instructed her lawyers accordingly. At least, it would be one less complication in my increasingly solitary existence.

Too travel-worn to go out to a restaurant, I extracted a frozen pizza from the freezer, added additional cheese, canned sweet corn and anchovies and put it into the microwave. While the end product was quite acceptable in an emergency, I couldn't help thinking how I'd much rather be sitting down to a meal of battered haddock and a dish of mixed vegetables, Northern-style. Medically imprudent they might be, but as the man said, you have to die of something.

And to paraphrase what the other man said, battered haddock corrupts, but battered haddock in beef dripping corrupts absolutely and, if I was to maintain my reputation as a leading professional gourmet and *bon vivant*, I would obviously have to hide my new addiction from the world. I opened a bottle of *Cabernet Sauvignon*, drank three glasses in rapid succession and went to bed.

꿏

Actor-cleaner Maggie Turnbull turned up the following morning, took in my doleful expression and, over a cup of coffee, said casually:

'None of my business, but what happened to your little friend?'

'My little friend?'

'The one who opened the door to me last time I was here. Pretty little thing in a see-through nightie. Gone back to France has she?'

Having had to communicate with my house-guest (with great difficulty, as it turned out) without any prior warning, she was entitled to some sort of explanation and I gave her a brief summary of the sequence of events.

She nodded and said: 'I thought it must have been something like that. She didn't seem to be your type.'

Purely out of curiosity, I asked: 'What do you think my type is?'

'Not a little flibberty-gibbet like her. Some one a little older, with a good head on her shoulders. She'd have to be physically attractive, of course - like Mrs Tomlinson in number 27, for example.'

I was slightly taken-aback:

'You know her?'

'Of course I know her. She's a client. She told Daphne and Deirdre she needed a cleaner and they got on to Binkie, who sent me.'

'Ah,' I said: 'Well, you're quite right in one way. I do agree she's a very attractive woman. But unfortunately, as far as she's concerned, I'm *persona non grata*.'

She drained her coffee cup and rose to her feet:

'Yes, well, like I said, it's none of my business. So I won't ask you why.'

'I wish you would,' I said, earnestly.

It would be nice to talk to some one - anyone - to help get Geneviève out of my system and Maggie Turnbull was as good a listener as one could hope for. She made herself another mug of coffee and said nothing until I'd finished relating the series of events that had resulted in me being branded (not unreasonably, I hasten to admit) as a married adulterer who had imported his French fancy-woman to Muswell Hill. The fact that Michelle was now a married woman and that I was in the process of getting a divorce, seemed irrelevant.

Her reaction was simple, to the point and as frank as

Deirdre's and Daphne's:

'Dam' fool. What are you going to do about it?'

'Not a lot I can do about it.'

'Rubbish. There's always something to be done.'

'Like what?'

An abrupt: 'I'll think about it.'

The cup was drained, the carpet slippers replaced by her *Doc Martens* and she was gone. Strangely, I suddenly felt less socially-reclusive and less full of self-pity and when, later that day, the telephone rang and Mr Phipps asked me to accompany him to take part in quiz night at one of the local public houses, I accepted immediately. It was to prove yet another interesting experience.

Though it was my first visit to a public house since I was last in England as a young man, far too many years ago, I soon discovered that the traditional English pub had changed a great deal. And not, according to Mr Phipps, for the better. Gone were the cosy country-style inns of the past, where the locals could enjoy a pint of warm beer in Spartan surroundings, with creaking wooden chairs, unsteady tables, sawdust on bare floorboards and ageing ham rolls as the only food on offer. Also no longer in evidence were the old oak beams that had supported smoke-blackened ceilings for many years and which had been placed at exactly the right height to come into contact with the skull of many an unwary customer.

Instead, complained Mr Phipps, the men in suits from the breweries, with their fancy degrees in business management, had come to the conclusion that the way forward was to transform - or "poncify," as he put it - good old-fashioned

151

taverns into so-called theme pubs, in an attempt to attract a younger, more free-spending clientele.

As a result, said Mr Phipps, traditional old English country taverns that had been part of the fabric of Muswell Hill since it was a little village, with names like *The Cock, The Bull* and *The Old Dun Cow*, had all been given a makeover. Hostelries where it had once been possible for a customer to sit for hours over a single half-pint of mild-and-bitter, while just staring vacantly into space, had all been turned into centrally-heated, softly-illuminated, fully-carpeted establishments with a wide choice of food, padded chairs, giant television screens and background music. Worst of all, the old inn signs had been taken down and each pub given a new name.

'Now I ask you,' said Mr Phipps as we walked along the Broadway - or rather as I walked and he hobbled, on his plastered foot: 'Why should anyone want to patronise a pub called *The Slug and Cabbage*, which is not a million miles from where we're now standing?'

He stubbed his toe against the kerb and gave a yelp of pain:

'One day, I'll swing for that old git. I thought I was on to him, but he got me with his second bowl.'

As we continued on our way, he built up a head of steam against the iniquities of latter-day breweries:

'I mean, who in their right mind would want to eat in a pub with a name like *The Slug and Cabbage*? Even the thought of a bloody great slug on a cabbage leaf makes me want to throw up.'

As the evening wore on, I discovered that to Mr Phipps, most things appeared to be bloody, in one way or another. He shook his head in wonderment:

'And d'you know what they're going to call *The Old*

White Lion? A feller at the bowls club told me it's going to be changed to *The Toad and Testicle*. Can you bloody believe it?'

Frankly, I couldn't. And I told him so.

He considered for a moment, then nodded: 'You're probably right. It is a bit OTT, isn't it?'

'OTT?'

'Over the top. Yes, even those berks from the brewery wouldn't come up with a name like that. He must have been winding me up.'

'Winding you up?'

'Extracting the Michael.'

'Extracting the Michael?'

'Taking the - ' He shook his head in irritation: 'Look. You really should learn to speak proper English.'

He was quite right, of course. And it occurred to me that after a couple of hours in Mr Phipps' company, I'd have little need for a language school.

'Well, whatever they're going to call it, it's all a bloody disgrace. And I'll tell you this, the breweries have lost a lot of custom from people like me.'

Perhaps, I thought, somewhat cynically, that was the whole idea. But my companion saw it from a different viewpoint.

'Oh yes, they're going to rue the day they banned customers like me who, when they'd had a couple, liked to entertain their fellow punters with a couple of choruses of *Nellie Dean*. Now, all they allow you to do is put money into their karaoke machines and sing-a-long-a-Sinatra, doing it his bloody way.' His disapproval was almost tangible: 'I wouldn't be going to their quiz night tonight, if there wasn't the possibility of us walking out at the end of the evening showing a profit.'

We entered the pub and Mr Phipps accepted my offer of a drink:

'Thanks. A half of bitter's my usual tipple, but what with my foot giving me gip, I wouldn't say no to a double scotch.' He adopted a suitably pathetic expression: 'It might help to ease the pain.'

As it turned out, he didn't say no to a double scotch for the rest of the evening. He left me at the bar and took his place at a centre table to await the other members of our little group. It seemed that at quiz nights, success was far more likely if you took part as one of a small team. In that way, individual specialist knowledge could be shared with the others, with the proceeds from a winning quiz card being equally divided between the members of the group.

'And even split five ways,' said Mr Phipps, as he sipped his double scotch: 'It's still worth having - especially when the prize money has been rolled over, like it has been for the past three weeks. There's now over two hundred quid in the pot.' He nodded towards a group of drinkers at a corner table who were whispering amongst themselves: 'That's why the quiz team from *The Flag & Ferret* are here. They're after our jackpot. Cheeky sods.'

'Who are the other members of our team?'

'Shane, Arthur and Enid. They'll be here any minute. I invited you because what with you being French and foreign and that, you must be good at answering questions about foreign parts, not to mention ones on food and wine, right?' He glanced towards the door: 'Ah. Here they are now.'

He gulped down his scotch in a single swallow and pointedly placed the empty glass in front of him, presumably in the hope that one of the new arrivals would notice it and offer to have it filled up. The hope proved to be somewhat forlorn.

'My shout,' said the small man in glasses with thinning hair, a blood-stained bandage on thumb and forefinger and an ancient sports jacket. To Mr Phipps, he said: 'The usual, Wilfred?'

Mr Phipps indicated his empty whisky glass and said: 'Well actually - '

'The usual it is,' said the small man, swiftly. He'd obviously been there before.

'This is Arthur,' growled Mr Phipps: 'He's our crafts, hobbies and woodwork expert. That's what he teaches at *The Clement Attlee Comprehensive*, over in Wood Green.'

Arthur offered me a hand that carried the scars of a thousand slipped chisels and departed in the direction of the bar, while Phipps introduced me to the second member of the team - a rather dowdy, but pleasant-faced, middle-aged woman, wearing a shapeless woollen dress and a knitted hat. The hand she extended bore the inky traces of a malfunctioning ballpoint pen.

'Enid's literature and the arts - she's the secretary of the *Colney Hatch Writers' Circle* and she owns a full set of *Encyclopedia Brittanica*.'

'And I've read every one of them,' she said, modestly.

I was very impressed. While I've known many people who were in possession of a full set of *Encyclopedia Brittanicas*, she was the very first person I'd met who had actually read even one of them. Of course, how much she remembered from what she had read, remained to be seen.

'And finally,' said Mr Phipps, indicating the rather Neanderthal-looking young man with a shaven head and an imposing beer-belly: 'This is Shane.'

Shane was dressed in a baseball hat and a grubby T-shirt that proclaimed *Elvis is Alive and Well and Living in Crouch*

End. By his appearance and the way he communicated in grunts rather than normal speech, I would have thought that his general knowledge would be rather limited, if not non-existent.

I was wrong.

Said Mr Phipps: 'Shane's speciality is sport. He's a genius at sport is Shane, football in particular. There's nothing he doesn't know about soccer. You can recite the names of every FA cup winner since the game began, can't you Shane?'

The genius gave a nod and a grunt and took a seat. Somewhat uncharitably, I couldn't help wondering if he could also recite the names of every football hooligan since the game began. After all, he could certainly pass for one. Enid took the seat next to mine.

'I'm also quite knowledgeable about local matters,' she volunteered, shyly: 'For example, the term "booby hatch" - or lunatic asylum, came into being when the Victorians built the largest institution for the insane in England, just off Colney Hatch Lane. What's more,' she added eagerly: 'It had the longest corridor in Europe - almost a mile long. Not a lot of people know that.'

I certainly didn't. And when I was further informed that the site of the asylum had since been converted into up-market houses and apartments, I realised this plethora of useless information might well prove to be very helpful at a pub quiz night. In short, Mr Phipps seemed to have assembled a well-balanced, if rather motley, team of competitors and I was quite looking forward to joining in.

A single quiz card cost one English pound and we each

bought three. With fifteen different cards between us, Mr Phipps reckoned we were in with a chance. Each card, he informed me, carried a different set of numbers - similar to *Bingo, Lotto* and *Housey-Housey* cards. After the quizmaster had drawn a number out of a hat, he would then ask a question and everyone with that number on their quiz card would try to write down the answer. And the first one to succeed in filling up his or her card with all-correct answers, would be declared the winner. To me, it seemed a little complicated, but to the many participants who packed the pub and who were gazing fixedly at their cards, pencils poised, it seemed to be all in a night's work.

'Watch that lot on the left,' muttered Mr Phipps: 'They're from *The Goose & Firkin*, in Highgate. As soon as they heard this week's jackpot was over two hundred quid, like them in the corner, they came here mob-handed with a couple of mobile phones.'

'Mobile phones?' I said: 'What have they got to do with it?'

'You'll see,' said Mr Phipps darkly: 'Now where's the bloody quizmaster?'

The bloody quizmaster turned out to be the portly, rather bored-looking landlord, or mine host (as I gather he was called in happier, pre theme-pub days) who instructed the barmaids to turn down the music. He then switched on the microphone, blew into it, said 'testing, testing,' for no apparent reason and launched into the first of the 20-odd questions:

'Number six on your cards.'

'I've got a six,' said Mr Phipps.

'Me too,' said Arthur.

'I haven't,' said Enid.

'Me neither,' said Shane.

Neither had I.

Said the quizmaster: 'Question six on your cards. What was the name of Mozart's wife? I will repeat that: What was the name of Mozart's wife?'

Our team did not get off to an auspicious start.

'No idea,' said Arthur.

'Me neither,' said Enid.

'Haven't a clue,' said Mr Phipps.

'Who the hell's Mozart?' muttered Shane.

'A German composer,' I said.

'We all know that,' said Mr Phipps, testily: 'Well, nearly all of us. But who was his trouble and strife?'

Said Arthur: 'We'll have to go back to that one, during the break.'

'Hold on,' said Shane: 'Mozart's wife? That's easy.'

We all looked at him in some surprise. Shane lowered his voice, leaned forward and said proudly:

'Gotta be Mrs Mozart, right?'

'I doubt it, Shane,' said Arthur, kindly, as if addressing a retarded orang-utan: 'I don't think that's the answer he's looking for.'

The retarded orang-utan looked quite put-out:

'Anyone think of a better one?'

No one could.

'There you are then,' said Shane triumphantly.

Once again, I reflected, what had started out as a promisingly normal social intercourse was, as usual, starting to lurch into the surreal. That pattern of dialogue continued through the evening, until the landlord quizmaster called a break. According to a disgruntled Mr Phipps, who had yet to write down one single answer, this was to allow the competitors to jettison the amount of alcohol they'd consumed over the previous hour or so, which, in turn, would enable them to knock back a few more gallons of over-priced wines, beer and spirits - the sole reason, muttered Mr Phipps, for the brewery running a quiz night in the first place.

He was not the happiest of men and I was beginning to wonder how many of his acquaintances, after a few hours in his company, felt an almost irresistible urge to jump off the nearest high building. It was only then that I noticed both Arthur and Enid going through the door that led to the pub carpark, each clutching a wad of quiz cards.

'Where are they off to?' I asked Mr Phipps.

'Where d'you think?' he said.

In transpired that during the break, the carpark became the scene of a large number of competitors, each shouting urgently into their mobile phone to someone at the other end who was undoubtedly sitting at home surrounded by reference books, all trying desperately to find the answers to the questions that were still to be resolved. The use of mobile phones within the pub during the quiz was banned - if only because a cacophony of competitors bawling down their mobiles might upset the others.

'Enid's phoning her daughter, who's got all her *Brittanicas* in front of her and Arthur's phoning his dad. The old boy might be a bit senile, but he's got total recall for anything that happened before 1939. Course,' continued Mr Phipps: 'You've got to have a bit of luck as well as knowing all the answers - like having the right numbers on your card in the first place.'

'Time they were back on the field,' grunted Shane, football obviously conditioning his every thought: 'The whistle's about to blow for the second half.'

'Her name was Anna Marie,' whispered Enid as she sat down at the table, glancing around the room to make sure she hadn't been overheard.

'Whose was?' asked Shane.

'Mozart's wife,' hissed Mr Phipps, filling in the empty space on his quiz card.

'And Oliver Cromwell had a wart on his nose,' whispered Arthur: 'Dad remembered seeing a picture of him at Kenwood House, in 1938.'

Kenwood House, Enid informed me, was an elegant Georgian mansion house that had been built on the upper reaches of nearby Hampstead Heath and which had since been converted into a centre for music and the arts, including a portrait gallery.

For the first time that evening, Mr Phipps looked almost cheerful:

'Well, all we need now is a few questions on food, wine, football and lawn green bowling and we're in with a chance.'

Sadly, the questions never came and those that did, much to our chagrin, failed to match the numbers on our cards, even though between us - and this was the most frustrating part - we happened to know most of the answers.

'Sod's law,' muttered Arthur, as he drained his pint and rose to his feet.

'I wouldn't mind,' said Mr Phipps, quite untruthfully, I suspect: 'If the jackpot had been won by one of our regulars. But to watch those bastards from *The Goose and Firkin* walking off with over two hundred quid of our money really pisses me off - oh sorry Enid.'

'My sentiments entirely,' said Enid graciously. And turning to me, she said: 'Might I have a little word with you, Pierre?'

'Of course.'

'You being a professional writer who's actually had his name in print, I wonder if you'd be kind enough to address our little writing circle and present our annual awards in October? It would be most appreciated by our members.'

Even though I pointed out that I was merely a journalist, not a writer of fiction, poetry or any of the other forms of creative endeavour, she was quite insistent that the mere presence of a published writer would inspire them all to greater things. How could I refuse? While Mr Phipps and I were both considerably out of pocket, I had enjoyed the evening, if only because it had succeeded in taking my mind off my other problems. We made our way back to *Arcadia Court* and parted at the lift. But as went our separate ways, Mr Phipps' parting shot was like a stab to the heart:

'See you at Mrs Whatsit's flat-warming party on Friday, right?'

Wrong, I thought sadly, the misery flooding back. But when I opened the door to my apartment, I was surprised to find a small pink envelope on the inside mat. On opening it, I found a neatly printed invitation to Geneviève Tomlinson's house-warming party, for the following Friday evening. This was accompanied by a short, hand-written note in which she deeply apologised for having behaved so insensitively when confronted with my young French house-guest and hoped that my current difficulties, distressing though they might be, would soon be resolved satisfactorily. Pleased but perplexed, I wondered what had prompted her to write such a note.

I was to soon to discover why.

I was completing my piece detailing the fleshpots of

Lancashire and Yorkshire when the doorbell rang. I opened the door to be confronted by actor-cleaner Maggie Turnbull.

'As I was in the building - it's my day to do for Deirdre and Daphne - just thought I'd pop in to ask if you've heard from Mrs Tomlinson.'

'Well, yes, I have actually. But how did you know?'

'Yesterday, your name came up while I was washing her kitchen floor and I happened to mention I was getting rather worried about you.'

'Worried about me? In what way?'

'The way you were so unhappy on account of your bitch of a wife having dumped you for someone else.'

'I was?'

'Of course you were. That's why you're in the process of divorcing her.'

'I am? Yes, of course I am.'

'And that you were absolutely heart-broken. So much so, I thought you might do something silly.'

'Something silly? Like what?'

Maggie sighed: 'Really Pierre, I do wish you wouldn't repeat everything I say. You're beginning to sound like a constipated parrot.'

'Sorry.'

'But no matter how distressed you were, you still went out of your way to give a helping-hand to a naive little French girl from your home village who'd been seduced by her gentleman friend and was now carrying his child.'

'I did?'

'Of course you did. What's more, you persuaded this man to do the right thing and marry the girl. Which he did.'

'He did? Yes, of course he did. And she believed all this?'

'Why shouldn't she? It's all true, isn't it?'

'Well, sort of.'

'Of course she believed it. I'm an actress, for heaven's sake and I can head-clutch with the best of them. The woman was nearly in tears by the time I'd finished.' Maggie seemed inordinately proud of herself: 'Say it though I do myself, I did give quite a performance. Anyway, you're *persona grata* again, all right?'

'I just don't know what to say, Maggie.'

'Say nothing. I told you I'd come up with something. And I enjoyed every minute of it.' She glanced at her watch: 'Must rush. Got to go for an open audition at the *Regents Park Theatre*. They're looking for some one to play *Mother Courage*. Won't get it, of course. I look about as motherly as *Attila the Hun*. But it's all good practice.' She gave me a brief smile and a nod: 'Have fun at the flat-warming.'

I did.

OCTOBER

THE SUN SHONE IN OCTOBER. At least, it did for me, as the adorable Geneviève Tomlinson, to my utter astonishment, intimated that she was willing to lend me a shoulder to weep on, in my hour of need, before having to depart on an extended visit to a French-speaking, North African country, where she would act as interpreter to a senior British trade minister.

I remember little of her flat-warming party, just the way she took me aside and greeted me with genuine warmth mixed with obvious concern. Maggie Turnbull must have laid it on with a *bêche*. Geneviève first looked at me anxiously, as if checking for signs of me having contemplated hurling myself off the roof of Alexandra Palace, then said, gently:

'I do know what you're going through, Pierre. I've been through it myself and I do apologise for jumping to the wrong conclusions. I should have realised that you couldn't possibly be that sort of person.' She placed her hand over mine: 'But no matter how down you might feel at the moment, things will work out, believe me. They always do.' She squeezed my hand reassuringly: 'What you need is someone to take you out of yourself - in the same way you took me out of myself, at the barbecue. I'll never forget how kind you were to a very unhappy, very lonely new resident and the way in which you made me feel so very, very welcome.'

I looked at her, blankly. Kind? To my shame, after all those months of celibacy since leaving Ménerbes (apart from the unexpected one-night-stand with the fearsome librarian from the *St Catherine's School for Girls*), from the moment I first saw Geneviève, my thoughts were purely carnal. I wanted to sweep her up in my arms, mount an imaginary white stallion and gallop off with her into the desert or, failing that, a secluded corner of Alexandra Park. It was her sweetness, tinged with sadness, that made me silently berate myself for even thinking such things and from that moment on, I was utterly lost.

And now my feelings were apparently being reciprocated. Why? What on earth could she possibly see in me? An attractive, high-flying woman like her and me, a middle-ranking French food, wine and travel writer who'd never make the sort of money that would keep a woman like her in the state to which she must have become accustomed. While I wasn't bad looking, Adonis I wasn't. It was all very confusing. And all rather wonderful.

'Yes, well, there's no accounting for taste,' said Deirdre, when I dropped in for coffee the following morning and told them that Geneviève and I were going out to dinner that same evening.

'No logic to it,' agreed Daphne: 'Either you go for some one or you don't. It's a sort of chemical thing - as I know to my cost. You can't imagine the sort of men I used to get the hots for - for no apparent reason.'

'No apparent reason?' scoffed Deirdre: 'You used to get the hots for any man with a thick enough wallet and a big enough - '

'Not in front of our guest,' said Daphne quickly: 'Anyway, Pierre, by the way Geneviève was looking at you at the party, she obviously fancies you rotten.'

'So just lie back and enjoy it,' advised Deirdre: 'While it lasts.'

'Why shouldn't it last?'

'For one thing,' said Daphne: 'She's off to foreign parts in a few days and won't be back for months. And anything could happen during that time.'

'Anything,' agreed Deirdre, with a wicked grin: 'Perhaps she'll meet some one else. An Arab sheikh, for instance, who'll offer her boss a couple of camels and the odd bunk-up with a few of his wives, if he throws in Geneviève as part of the trade agreement.'

'I wish you wouldn't keep trying to cheer me up,' I said gloomily: 'I'm worried enough as it is.'

'We're just teasing you, Pierre,' said Daphne: 'Even though she hardly knows you and you hardly know her, we reckon you're it. Whether you like it or not. And once a woman's made up her mind...'

I felt a little better after that.

'So be a good lad while she's away,' said Deirdre sternly: 'Because that'll be the testing time. You don't mess about with a woman like Geneviève.'

'I have no intention of messing about with anyone,' I said coldly. *Mon Dieu*, I was besotted with the woman. As in the movie of the same name, I was *Truly, Madly, Deeply* in love. For the very first time in my life.

'Just as well,' said Daphne: 'Because we happen to like her very much and we'll be keeping our beady little eyes on you.'

'Please do,' I said, wondering how I was going to be able to get through the next few months without *ma belle Geneviève* and I resolved to make her few remaining days in England as agreeable as I could.

؇

After all those months of dining alone, all in the line of duty, it was most refreshing to share a table with an exquisite woman and woo her with the finest food and wines in London - with the added satisfaction of knowing that *Le Courrier's* accountants would be picking up the bill. It was during those delightful dinners, at the most fashionable and expensive of venues, that I began to learn a little more about my amoureuse.

I was already aware that she was the product of a French mother and an English father and it emerged that when they'd first met, her father was a young medical student and her mother a trainee midwife, at the then internationally-famed Waterloo Lying-In Hospital in London, which taught the gynaecological complexities of midwifery to students from all over the world. It seemed that their hands had accidentally touched while she was assisting him to administer an epidural and that, apparently, had been that. Echoing what Daphne had said, it must have been a chemical thing and some time later, they were married by special license. A few months after that, she'd been obliged to book her own bed in the very same hospital, in advance of the birth of what turned out to be a daughter.

Sadly, Geneviève Tomlinson's parents parted when she was just a few years old. Her mother had tried her hardest to make the marriage work, but the combination of hardly ever seeing her hard-working husband and the continually depressing English climate drove her back to her beloved Provence, taking their daughter with her. The parting had been amicable and as soon as she was old enough to travel on her own, Geneviève had been happily shuttled between mother and father, which explained her faultless French and English

'Provence?' I said in amazement: 'Your mother came from Provence?'

'A little village called Lacoste, in the Lubéron.'

'How extraordinary. My home's in Ménerbes. That's just a few kilometres away.'

'I know it well, Pierre.'

We both fell silent for a moment, pondering upon the significance of having so much in common. But there was still one question I needed to have answered.

'Your husband. This... Mr Tomlinson. What was he - what is he - like?'

'He's someone I met when I was very young. When I was teaching French at *The Berlitz School of Languages*, in Oxford Street. We weren't an item then, but when we bumped into each other a few years later, he was a junior civil servant at the Foreign Office and I was on its team of translators.'

Seething with jealousy, I said: 'I suppose he's tall, blonde, suave and handsome, with an impeccable upper-class pedigree.'

She looked at me in some surprise: 'Well no, he's rather on the short side, actually. With receding hair and the beginnings of a paunch. And his father was a bus driver from

Balham. Not that it mattered what his father was. Colin was bright enough to win a scholarship to Oxford and was invited to apply to join the civil service.'

'That still doesn't explain - '

She laid a gentle finger across my lips and said:

'And please don't ask me why I married him. I've been asking myself the same question from the moment we walked out of the Registry Office. I suppose I just felt sorry for him. He always seemed so... lost and out of his depth at the F.O. He was simply in the wrong job.' She toyed with her wine glass and shook her head, unhappily: 'We were never very close. We had so little in common. And we just drifted apart. Even so, it's sad to go through a divorce. Any divorce.'

I had a feeling of intense relief. That explained it all. She'd married him out of pity, out of concern. In other words, she was a woman of great compassion for life's walking wounded, a compulsive collector of lame dogs and... *Mon Dieu!* I thought. Is that why she's being so kind to me? Because she sees me as a pathetic nonentity? At that moment, as if reading my mind, she leaned across the table, placed her hand over mine and said, softly:

'If I wasn't leaving in the morning, I wouldn't be saying this. But I just want you to know that from the moment I first saw you, I felt like a young girl again. You made me go quite weak at the knees, Pierre. Yes, really. I don't know why and I don't want to know why. All I do know is, I think I've fallen in love. I say *think*, because it's far too early to know for sure. And I don't want to make the same mistake twice. But if I still feel the same way about you by the time I get home from North Africa, well, you'd better look out.' She gave a wry little smile: 'Now, if I've scared you half to death, this is the moment to make a run for it.'

I took a deep breath and said, quite foolishly: 'When you say you think you've fallen in love, you mean with me?'

'No, of course not, you *idiot de Français*. With Malcolm Nesbitt.' She squeezed my hand even tighter: 'Now don't you think it's about time we went to bed?'

It was. And we did.

∞

It was hard to say goodbye to her. Our first (and hopefully, not our last) night together had been a memorable experience and having to say *au revoir chérie*, to a woman who seemed close to tears, was something very new to me. I'd known tears of rage from my wife and tears of self-pity from Michelle, but this show of genuine *tristesse* was very touching.

'I'll write,' she called, as she pushed her luggage trolley towards the *Passengers Only* doorway at London's Heathrow Airport. A final little smile and she was gone.

Heavy of heart, I returned home to Muswell Hill, feeling lonelier than at any other time since I'd arrived in England. Would she still feel the same way about me when she returned? Who could tell? I had never been convinced that absence, as they say, made the heart grow fonder. *Absinthe*, yes. In the short term. And if administered in liberal quantities. So all I could do is wait. And hope.

Again, I told myself that the best way of coping with such feelings was to bury myself into my work and become involved with every social activity on offer. I soon discovered that with the onset of autumn and the nights starting to draw in, the English reluctantly pack away their bowls, gardening tools and barbecues and seek new ways of passing the time until the first signs of spring. Winter hobbies and pastimes flourish, usually in the shape of specialised clubs and societies. Indeed, the first day of October invariably signals an explosion of activity in the heady world of amateur dramatics, when rehearsals begin for every sort of production - from Aldous Huxley's depressing-but-worthy *Giaconda Smile* to the ever popular *Student Prince*.

At the local Adult Education Institutes, night-school courses abound, catering for those with an urge to master the art of origami, finger-painting or *petit-point*. Aero-modelling clubs are also thick on the ground, where the members spend most of the winter months lovingly constructing their fragile model aircraft which, on their maiden flights, usually end up as mangled piles of balsa wood, glue and fabric, after crashing into the grounds of Alexandra Park. But my first excursion into the realms of self-entertainment (if it can be called that) had already been agreed and a telephone call from Enid of Mr Phipps' pub quiz-night team, reminded me that I'd promised to present the annual awards at *The Colney Hatch Writers' Circle*, to be held in a local church hall, the following Thursday.

'Our usual routine is this,' said Enid, as she briefed me before the members were due to arrive: 'First, members are invited to give a reading of their latest work, then, after a frank discussion and criticism by the other members of the *Writers' Circle*, the guest of honour makes a short address and announces the winners.'

'Who decides who the winners are?'

'You do.'

'Me?

'Of course. You're the only one with no axe to grind.'

Had I known beforehand what would be expected of me, I very much doubt if I would have accepted Enid's invitation. For one thing, I really wasn't qualified to judge any form of literary endeavour, apart from newspaper feature writing. For another, I had no wish to face the slings and arrows of outrageous - or rather outraged - writers, who hadn't won a prize. But it was too late to back out now.

'Very well,' I said: 'What are the prizes, by the way?'

'Oh, nothing very special,' said Enid: 'Just the odd bottle of wine or a matching pen and pencil set. Things like that. It's the certificate that's the most important - the one every winner gets, signed by the President and praising their literary achievements.'

'The President?'

'The Reverend Dennis Aspinall. He's had his name in print lots of times. Mostly in the *St. Margaret's Church Magazine* which, of course, he writes himself. But that does make him the nearest thing to a professional writer that we've got.'

The Reverend Aspinall turned out to be a pleasant, if rather rumpled-looking clergyman in his 60s, with a vague smile, a somewhat grubby dog-collar and an expression of perceptual surprise, as if not quite sure what he was doing presiding over such a motley group of would-be novelists, poets, television playwrights and short-story writers. And motley they were. Middle-aged ladies in hand-knitted hats, kaftan dresses and wooden beads; several men of indeterminate age, some in fishermen's jerseys and open-toed sandals - and a clutch of nervously-giggling young women, whose ambitions seemed to be more social than literary.

The objects of their interest appeared to be the handful of

young men, all looking very intense and serious and all seemingly clutching a film or television script. The young women were obviously intent on being around and available should any one of them hit the financial big-time and end up on a sun-lounger by the side of a swimming pool in Hollywood. While there are, of course, similar amateur literary societies in France these, I was told, bear no comparison with those in England, where half the population now seems to be a member of one writing group or another.

Explained Enid: 'We used to be a little group of a couple of dozen or so, but since J. K. Rowling hit the jackpot with *Harry Potter*, everyone wants to have a go at writing. That little bastard in a pointy hat has a lot to answer for.'

Which presumably explained why, among the members taking their seats, was a most unlikely quartet from *Arcadia Court*: Mr Phipps, Mrs Betty Ballard from the first floor front and, on the arm of her son, the stoney-faced Mrs Nesbitt. Thankfully, on this occasion, little Alice was not in attendance.

Trailing reluctantly behind them was the occupant of the second floor back, a morose, middle-aged man named Sharples whom I had met only once before - and fleetingly at that - at Malcolm Nesbitt's barbecue, where we'd merely nodded to each other over a chicken drumstick. It transpired that Mr Sharples (or 'Dickie' as Mr Phipps insisted upon calling him, much to Sharples' obvious annoyance) - was, by profession, a literary agent. Dickie, which I understand is the English diminutive for Richard, had been constrained by Enid into attending The Circle's annual awards night in the hope of discovering an exciting new talent who would then be in need of an agent. But as the evening progressed, from Sharples' permanently pained expression as he listened to the various offerings, it would appear that Enid's hopes were rather forlorn.

I took my seat on the platform next to the Reverend Aspinall and Enid, the Writers' Circle secretary, brought the meeting to order. She then introduced me as their special guest, wildly exaggerating my writing credentials to such an extent that it even evinced a flicker of interest from *Arcadia Court's* very own literary agent. Then after somewhat rashly promising everyone an exciting and stimulating evening, she declared the annual awards night to be officially open.

Malcolm Nesbitt was the first to be called to the platform to read out his new work for the consideration and criticism of his fellow members. Which was simply the beginning of an evening that became increasingly bizarre. With an encouraging nod from his mother, Malcolm gave a nervous little smile, cleared his throat and announced:

'"*It's Mushroom Time at Alexandra Palace.*' *A personal experience in verse, by M. Nesbitt.*' He took a deep breath, peered at the piece of lined paper which seemed to have been torn from a school exercise book and launched into his ode:

'It's mushroom time at Alexandra Palace.
And Malcolm Nesbitt went down with Alice,
It's terrible hard to sniff out fungi,
Especially on a rainy Sunday,
At the Palace,
With Alice.
But lo, behold, what did she see -?'

We were never to discover what Alice saw, as Malcolm was interrupted in full flow by a large, middle-aged lady in a hessian dress, wooden-hoop ear-rings, a doughnut-bun hairstyle and a severe expression:

'Point of order, Mr President. I was under the impression

that all work submitted here tonight had to be an *original* piece of writing, am I not correct?'

Mr President looked bemusedly at Enid. She nodded.

'It appears so, Miss - er, Mrs - er, madam.'

'In that case, may I point out to you and to the meeting as a whole that M. Nesbitt's piece seems to be merely a re-workng of A.A. Milne's famous poem *They're Changing the Guard at Buckingham Palace*? The one where Christopher Robin goes down there with his nursemaid, who's also called Alice.'

An uneasy Mr President turned to Malcolm and said: 'Mr. Nesbitt?'

Said Malcolm, defensively: 'It's true to say that I have always been influenced by A.A. Milne - I've still got my Pooh Bear - but all writers are influenced by some one, aren't they? And if you're suggesting I've plagiarised him - '

'I'm afraid that is what I am suggesting, Mr. Nesbitt,' said the large lady: 'And while I accept that you could have done it subconsciously, I do think the matter should be put to the vote.'

Bawled an unidentified voice from the back of the hall: 'He's pinched someone else's name, too. Her who wrote *The Railway Children*.'

'Point of information,' said Enid: 'That was E. Nesbit.'

'Even so,' said the voice: 'I still think we should vote on it.'

'I second that,' said Mr Phipps from the second row: 'The poem's a total rip-off.'

I felt that familiar surge of *déjà-vu*. It seemed that Enid's local booby hatch was again open for business. Mr Phipps turned to face the other members:

'Who votes for M. Nesbitt's poem to be disqualified?'

A forest of hands shot up into the air and Mr President had no option but to ask Malcolm to return to his seat. As he did so, a furious Mrs Nesbitt gave Mr Phipps a look that could have melted a polar ice cap. It would obviously be a long time before he received another invitation to a Nesbitt *soirée*, to enjoy the delights of her creative *cuisine*. But on reflection, perhaps that was one of his reasons for objecting to Malcolm's banal little piece in the first place.

Why Malcolm had chosen to steal such a well-known poem was beyond me. While it was quite reprehensible of him, had it been me, I would have lifted a totally obscure poem from the many out-of-print Georgian poetry collections which abound in second-hand bookshops. The next contender was a young man in a green sports jacket and corduroy trousers clutching what turned out to be the pilot script for a television medical soap opera:

'"Angie St Clair, Night Nurse Extraordinary," by Norman C. Rogers.'

Norman C. Rogers wet his lips and launched into his opus. He seemed to speak in capital letters when reading the stage instructions and in upper-and-lower-case when reading the dialogue:

'SCENE ONE. INTERIOR, HOSPITAL CASUALTY DEPARTMENT. NIGHT.

BECAUSE OF A PILE-UP ON THE NEARBY MOTORWAY, CASUALTY IS AWASH WITH DEAD, DYING AND INJURED PATIENTS.

*YOUNG, HANDSOME, **DOCTOR JASON BENEDICT** IS TENDING A PATIENT WHOSE HEAD IS AT A VERY FUNNY ANGLE.*

*(**MEDICAL NOTE**: THE PATIENT IS SUFFERING*

FROM A SEVERE BROKEN NECK).

FROM HIS ANXIOUS EXPRESSION, WE REALISE EXACTLY WHAT IS GOING THROUGH DOCTOR BENEDICT'S MIND:

JASON (Thinks): Where's nurse Angie St Clair? She should have been here half an hour ago. How can we possibly cope without her?

*AT THAT MOMENT, THE DOORS AT THE END OF THE ROOM ARE FLUNG OPEN AND **NURSE ANGIE ST CLAIR** IS FRAMED DRAMATICALLY IN THE DOORWAY.*

*(**CHARACTER GUIDE**: ANGIE IS YOUNG, INCREDIBLY BEAUTIFUL WITH SOFT, BLONDE, SHOULDER-LENGTH HAIR, A VOLUPTUOUS FIGURE WITH LONG LEGS AND A LOVELY SMILE. THE DAUGHTER OF AN ENGLISH COUNTRY SQUIRE, SHE WAS EDUCATED AT A FAMOUS GIRLS' BOARDING SCHOOL, WHERE SHE WAS GAMES CAPTAIN, NETBALL CHAMPION AND VOTED THE MOST POPULAR GIRL IN SCHOOL. HER HOBBIES ARE TENNIS, HORSE-RIDING AND PLAYING THE PIANO AT OLD FOLKS' HOMES. THOUGH ANGIE IS A DEDICATED NURSE, SHE IS, ABOVE ALL, A WOMAN.)'*

While I knew little about the art of writing for television, I couldn't help wondering how the audience could possibly know what the handsome Doctor Jason Benedict was actually thinking, purely because of his facial expression. Similarly, how could a viewer successfully assimilate Nurse Angie St Clair's parentage, sporting achievements and her apparently compulsive urge to play the piano to geriatrics, just by seeing her framed in the doorway? But as Norman C. Rogers must have at least read a book on the subject, I obviously had to give him the benefit of the doubt.

The author continued:

'ANGIE TAKES IN THE SITUATION WITH ONE SWIFT, PROFESSIONAL GLANCE AND MOVES QUICKLY OVER TO DOCTOR BENEDICT.'

Norman C. Rogers' voice dropped a couple of octaves, as he said, basso:

'Nurse St Clair! Thank God you're here!'

His voice then became soft, husky and sexually-charged:

'I came as soon as I could, Doctor. I'll attend to this patient. You're needed elsewhere.'

'Thanks nurse. Now you're here, I really think we've got a chance of making it through the night.'

HE PLACES HIS EQUIPMENT INTO HER WILLING HANDS.'

I looked at the author in disbelief. He places his equipment into her willing hands? This had to be a tongue-in-cheek satire of all things soapy, *oui? Non.* He was totally serious. He turned a page and said:

'ANGIE LOOKS DOWN AT THE PATIENT WITH A SEVERE BROKEN NECK AND TURNS QUICKLY TO A PASSING AMBULANCE MAN:

'Mr. Pargiter? I need splints, cotton wool and lots of hot water, quickly!'

'Splints, cotton wool and lots of hot water coming up, Miss.'

ANGIE GENTLY SQUEEZES THE ELDERLY PATIENT'S HAND AND FIGHTS BACK A TEAR:

'Don't worry, old timer, we'll soon have you up-and-about again and twice as cheerful.'

By now I was open-mouthed in amazement. What sort of nurse would treat an obviously terminally ill patient with a handful of cotton wool, half a bucket of hot water and a splint? The script was insane. The writer was insane. Who had been his medical adviser, I wondered - Pinnochio? I was relieved to see that I was not the only one who found Norman C. Rogers' offering less than convincing. The equally open-mouthed Mr Sharples was staring fixedly towards the author with an expression of total incredulity. But Rogers was obviously not the sort of writer to be deterred by the facts and continued reading his script to the very end.

I waited confidentially for the storm of criticism for his effort by his fellow members, but much to my astonishment, it never came. And as the evening progressed, it emerged that *Angie St Clair, Night Nurse Extraordinary* was by no means the worst of a very bad lot. These included a magazine article by Mr Phipps on the subtleties of lawn green bowling called, appropriately enough, *Blood on the Green*, various one act plays, radio scripts and a handful of poems, some of which were little more than limericks and verging upon the obscene.

Perhaps the most interesting and revealing of all was the first chapter of a bodice-ripping novel by Mrs Betty Ballard of the first floor front, in which she obviously revealed the sexual frustrations of a lifetime and which drove a disapproving Mrs Nesbitt to instruct Malcolm to put his hands over his ears. The prize-giving went off without incident. I handed out the wine, the pen-and-pencil sets and the signed certificates to the winners, all of whom I had chosen on the basis of the level of derision (or the lack of it), from their fellow-members.

The meeting broke up with literary agent Sharples

scuttling quickly out into the night, before any would-be client could buttonhole him - least of all the medically-challenged Norman C. Rogers. I made a point of asking Enid to come for a drink at a local hostelry, as I had no wish to walk home to *Arcadia Court* in the company of the Nesbitts, Mr Phipps and Mrs Betty Ballard, none of whom had won a prize. Enid, once she'd forced a few gins-and-tonics down her throat, turned out to be extremely entertaining company and her bawdy repertoire of anecdotes *risquées* were to me, surprisingly but refreshingly out of character.

It was almost midnight when I got back to my apartment to find an e-mail message from my wife's lawyer, stating that I was required to sign some divorce papers in the presence of my own lawyer, in Ménerbes. Sadly, there was no message from Geneviève. This was as good a reason as any to embark upon my long-delayed trip back home and the following morning, I took the *Eurostar* to Aix-en-Provence.

NOVEMBER

IT WAS RAINING WHEN I GOT TO MÉNERBES. Not heavily, but a gentle, post-autumn downfall that washed away the dust of summer and at the same time, discouraged the tourists from over-staying their welcome. It felt strange to be walking down the main street again, towards *Chez Moi*. As I wandered through the village, while I still caught the occasional exchange in English from passers-by, these emanated from English and American permanent residents, who had presumably read the aforementioned book by the English writer (whose name still escapes me) about the joys of living in Provence and had decided to become a part of it.

As winter approached, however, I could not help wondering whether some of these new residents who had made the boat-burning decision to move to Ménerbes, were now having second thoughts. The weather in the Lubéron can be very cold, bleak and unforgiving during the winter months, cold enough, in fact, to freeze *les boules* off a *singe métallique*, to paraphrase that quaint old English expression.

I first dropped into the local *Poste de Police* to inform the *Gendarmerie* that I had returned for a few days, then progressed to my maison, to find the shutters still locked firmly into place, happily with no sign of an attempted break-in, either by my wife or a passing *voleur*. I opened up the house, turned on the central heating, aired a bed and set off to see the *Avocat*.

My lawyer worked from his house just off the main square, his entire staff comprised one elderly lady in the inevitable black dress, with white lace cuffs, a large Victorian broach on her left bosom and a pair of ancient *pince-nez,* through which she eyed the world with infinite suspicion. She and her employer were well matched. Monsieur Gérard was not what you could call a cheerful man. In the years that he had acted as my legal advisor, he had elevated gloom, despondency and pessimism to a fine art and when I took out my pen in readiness to sign the necessary papers, he shook his head, woefully:

'Are you sure you wish to go through with this divorce, Monsieur LaPoste? It could cost you dearly, you know.'

'Even though my wife has admitted adultery and her lover is an exceedingly rich man, who has agreed to pay my legal costs?'

A weary sigh and another shake of the head: 'That's what they may say now, but once they get in front of the *juge*, you may well find that they will say something entirely different. Especially if your wife's *Avocat* encourages her to claim half your property, plus financial support, as he undoubtedly will.'

I was, of course, well aware that in France, would-be divorcees are still required to appear before a *juge*, whose task it is to attempt a reconciliation before accepting that the marriage has irretrievably broken down and is obliged to grant a divorce. But I could not agree with lawyer Gérard's assessment of the situation.

'In that case,' I said boldly: 'I will refuse her a divorce which will mean she will have to live in sin for the rest of her life.'

Unlike the morose Gérard, I knew my wife and the last thing she would wish to be is a mistress, rather than a spouse. Apart from the social connotations, if she failed to make her current lover her husband, he would be legally free to seek other, younger *amoureuses*, whenever the fancy took him.

'I suppose that's one way of looking at it,' said Monsieur Gérard, grudgingly: 'But don't say I didn't warn you.'

'I won't,' I promised and signed the papers.

My polite nod to his steely-eyed assistant on my way out was met with a look of total disapproval. Perhaps she believed in the old adage that marriage was, or should be, forever. While I was perfectly prepared to accept such an arrangement as far as Geneviève Tomlinson was concerned, the thought of being permanently bound in holy-deadlock with my adulterous wife was one hair-shirt too many.

❧

As I walked into the market place, the shriek of surprise from Michelle bounced off the buildings and won the attention of most of the local shoppers.

'Pierre! Chéri!'

The Ménerbiennes watched with interest as the plump, heavily-pregnant young woman waddled quickly across the square and embraced me, with obvious enthusiasm. They watched with even more interest as her undertaker husband caught up with her and prised her arms from around my neck:

'Arrête, Michelle!' he hissed: 'The whole village is watching!' To me he gave a brief nod and a cold: 'Please excuse us, Monsieur LaPoste. I am well aware that you and

183

my wife are old... friends, but I do not feel such public displays of affection are appropriate, in the circumstances.'

I readily agreed with him. Michelle's predictably spontaneous and uninhibited welcome would have already had many of the onlookers wondering just whose child it actually was.

'Come and dine with us,' pleaded Michelle: 'This place is so dead after Muswell Hill and I want you to tell me everything you've been up to since I left.'

Until that moment, I had been intending to spend the next few days just lounging about the house and strolling along to the local *Bar-Bistro* to catch up with the local gossip. But by the way Gaston Lafarge was glaring at me, to the obvious interest of the other residents, I was in little doubt that the main subjects of such gossip would be me, Michelle and Lafarge himself.

'I'm sorry, Michelle,' I said untruthfully: 'But I'm booked to go back to London tonight. But thank you for your invitation. You too, Monsieur Lafarge. Most kind of you.'

Lafarge gave me an icy nod. His dislike was almost palpable: 'Another time, perhaps,' he lied.

He took his wife's arm and steered her back towards the funeral parlour. Had I been able to read the thought-balloon floating above his head, it would doubtless have said:

"Another time? Kiss my derrière, you bâtard."

Before she was hustled out of view, Michelle blew me a kiss and bawled: *'À bientôt Chéri!'* The crowd broke up, giving me knowing looks and whispering amongst themselves. Their morning's shopping had turned out to be unexpectedly entertaining and the only question left to be answered was: who would the child mostly resemble - Monsieur Lafarge or myself? At least it was something for them to chat about during the dark winter months.

Within the hour, I had re-packed my suitcases, closed up the house, informed the *gendarmerie* of my leaving and pointed my hire-car in the direction of Aix-en-Provence. In one way, I was not sorry to be going back to Muswell Hill. At least, it would be a great deal livelier than a small Provençal village in winter.

∾ৡৢ৾

'Oh, you're back Pierre,' said Daphne.

'Just in time for Guy Fawkes night,' said Deirdre.

I remembered reading something about a man called Guy Fawkes in the French edition of *Reader's Digest* many years ago, whom they had disapprovingly described as a 15th century English anarchist who had attempted to blow up the Houses of Parliament when it was jam-packed with politicians. From the lofty heights of Highgate, on what is now known as Parliament Hill, he had confidently awaited the sight and sound of a massive explosion from the direction of Westminster, just a few miles to the South.

Sadly, his confidence seemed to have been somewhat misplaced, for no matter how praiseworthy his intentions might have been - or not, depending upon one's opinion of politicians, then and now - the so-called gunpowder plot was exposed and the unfortunate Guy Fawkes and his fellow conspirators summarily executed.

After the failure of the conspiracy, the English peasants were instructed to celebrate their law-makers' survival by building a bonfire on which they would be required to burn an effigy of the ill-starred Guy Fawkes, presumably as a warning to other malcontents with similar ideas to keep their tinderboxes firmly in their pockets. Thus to this very day, each November 5th sees the building of bonfires, the making of grotesque man-sized effigies and the letting-off of fireworks.

'It's great fun.' said Daphne, as we took the lift to the fourth floor: 'The local council has a big fireworks display at Alexandra Palace - must cost the ratepayers a small fortune - but we like ours the best.'

'Yours?'

'Arcadia Court's own little bonfire. In the gardens - y'know, where the Nesbitts held their barbecue.'

'That reminds me,' said Deirdre: 'Have you heard from Geneviève?'

'Not unless she's left a message on my answering machine.'

'Poor Pierre,' said Daphne: 'You must feel very lonely.'

'So you will come, won't you?' said Deirdre.

'Come where?'

Deirdre sighed: 'The bonfire party, of course. Malcolm Nesbitt arranges it and we all chip in for the fireworks.'

'There'll be food, drink, fudge, parkin, treacle toffee and roast chestnuts.'

I hesitated. It seemed an odd combination of comestibles and, if Mrs Nesbitt was doing the cooking, I had no wish to end-up on a saline drip at the Whittington hospital. But as I had nowhere else to go, I decided to live dangerously:

'Very well,' I said.

'We always go to the Ally Pally do first,' said Daphne.

'After all, we're paying for it,' said Deirdre: 'So pick us up at seven o'clock sharp.'

We parted at the lift gates. I entered my apartment and went straight to my answering machine. There were no messages. While it had been only been a few days since

Geneviève had left for North Africa, all my self-doubts and insecurities came flooding back and I couldn't help wondering if Daphne had been nearer to the truth than she'd thought - and that Geneviève's boss was already in deep negotiation with an affluent Arab:

'Only two camels, Achmed? Oh come on. She's worth a lot more than that. How about three camels, a couple of goats and half a kilo of hashish?'

For God's sake grow up, I told myself.

But with a woman like Geneviève in the picture, I knew it wasn't going to be easy.

On the evening of November 5th, from my fourth floor apartment window, I could see the rash of small bonfires that had flared into life in back gardens and public open spaces, the moment dusk had descended. These were private affairs, attended by friends, neighbours and their children, the latter seemingly being encouraged to spend the previous few weeks foraging for materials which would provide the basis for these social conflagrations. This possibly explained the sudden disappearance of anything combustible in the immediate vicinity - be it empty wooden boxes from behind the local supermarkets, lumber from the nearby building sites, the garden fences of unparticipating neighbours and the odd park bench.

Additional monies for fireworks were raised by groups of children who had made a badly-stuffed effigy of Guy Fawkes, usually wearing a schoolboy's peaked cap, a torn pair of jeans and a *papier-mâché* mask. This was placed in an old perambulator, which was then wheeled to various busy corners along Muswell Hill Broadway, where the children accosted passers-by and demanded the traditional "Penny for the Guy." Unfortunately however, presumably due to the level of inflation since the year 1605, any person unwise enough to actually attempt to donate the aforesaid traditional penny would, in some cases, become the target of a stream of angry and highly-inventive abuse.

In France, of course, civic fireworks celebrations normally take place on the 14th of July, to mark the successful storming of *La Bastille*, the notorious Parisian penal establishment from which, it has been said, the brave revolutionaries freed a grand total of three bewildered prisoners. One of the most spectacular fireworks displays in France is provided by the burghers of Aix-en-Provence and I was looking forward to seeing how these compared with those arranged by the worthies of Haringey Council, at Alexandra Palace.

I collected Daphne and Deirdre, as instructed, on the dot of seven o'clock and we set-off, via Springfield Avenue, to join the crowds on the slopes and terraces of the Palace to wait for the first, explosive start to the evening.

It was a good display and, coupled with the pleasantly festive atmosphere of the occasion, it was, in my view, worth every penny of Haringey Council's largesse with their residents' money. Daphne and Deirdre clapped their hands and whooped with excitement at every rocket, starburst and canonade, like the little girls they once were, so many years ago. I found their bright-eyed wonderment quite touching and I could only hope that if or when I reached their age, I would still have the same passion for life and living as they obviously did.

The display over, we retraced our steps to *Arcadia Court* where, accompanied by the occasional yelp of pain from Malcolm Nesbitt as he attempted to ignite the bonfire without setting fire to himself, the party was just beginning to get under way. I nodded politely to the stoney-faced Mrs Nesbitt who pretended not to notice, obviously still blaming me for my part in her son's literary fall from grace. Even so, I gave a friendly little wiggle of my fingers in the direction of the seated Alice, who immediately snarled and bared her little pointy teeth. Mr Phipps waved a casual hand in greeting and opened a bottle of beer. I was surprised to see him there, after his slight contretemps with the Nesbitts at *The Colney Hatch Writers' Circle Annual Awards* night. But it transpired that, as in previous years, he was in charge of the fireworks, while Malcolm's job was to tend the bonfire and roast the traditional chestnuts in its embers.

I wondered where Malcolm had found the wood to assemble his quite impressive funeral pyre for the unfortunate Guy Fawkes and was informed that he and Alice had been scouring the grounds of Alexandra Park for the last six months, collecting all the autumnal dead branches that had fallen off the many trees - plus anything else they had come across that was ignitable, with a little help, of course, from a can of *kérosène*. This did not, however, explain the number of wooden boxes, planks of wood and pieces of broken furniture that also adorned Malcolm's bonfire.

Where, I wondered had he got them?

Again, Mr Phipps seemed to be able to read my thoughts:

'Yes, well, he nicks them, don't he? In the middle of the night. Off of other peoples' bonfires. He told me he's been doing that since he was a kid, the saucy little sod.'

Too late, I remembered the old furniture from my

apartment still stored in my garage and made a mental note to offer it to ageing juvenile delinquent Malcolm Nesbitt for next year's conflagration. If, of course, I was still here. Inexplicably, I felt a twinge of sadness as I suddenly realised this would probably be my first and last Guy Fawkes night in Muswell Hill. What, I wondered, was happening to me? I looked around at my friends, neighbours and acquaintances of *Arcadia Court* and knew I was going to miss them. Well, some of them. Which raised another question. Something that had been puzzling me for some time. Where were the children at a social gathering such as this? Surely there had to be some residents with family members under the age of 16, in an apartment block the size of *Arcadia Court*?

'Everyone was invited,' said the thought-reading Mr Phipps: 'But why should any kid want to go to a fireworks party full of old farts and crumblies when they've got so many other parties to choose from? Most of the churches have one, with free drinks and as many roast potatoes as you can eat. The priests and preachers see it as a way of getting more recruits - y'know, come and light a Roman candle for Jesus. And when they've had enough of that, our little local arsonists can always find an abandoned car to set fire to and dance around that.'

I rather got the impression that Mr Phipps had little time or sympathy for the young. But then, had it been otherwise, he would not be the Mr Phipps we all knew and... well, we all knew.

Most of the other residents were now in attendance and as I lit a pair of sparklers for the young-in-heart Daphne and Deirdre, a tight-lipped Mrs Betty Ballard from the first floor front sidled up to me and said, sourly:

'I couldn't believe who you awarded prizes to at the

awards night. The winners were rubbish. Every one of them.'

I had hoped that my brush with the would-be Great English Novelist of Muswell Hill had been a one-off event. I was mistaken.

'It was a very difficult choice,' I said truthfully. As she had said, none of them had any literary merit whatsoever: 'But as a matter of interest, ' I continued: 'Your own very... interesting contribution apart, which entries do you think should have won a prize?'

'I've just said - none of them. But I'll tell you this, if the book I'm working on now doesn't win a prize at next year's awards, I'll resign. It's the best thing I've ever done.'

As she had obviously intended, I fell neatly into the trap.

'Really,' I said politely, if foolishly: 'What is it about?'

The bonfire had now died down to its final embers and, punctuated by more yelps of pain from Malcolm Nesbitt as he attempted to extract the well-roasted chestnuts from the red-hot ashes, Mrs Ballard outlined the plot of her latest offering.

Somewhat predictably, *Those Without Shame, by Blanche Lamarr* (apparently one of Mrs Ballard's many *noms-des-plumes*), appeared to be a *pastiche* of every heavy-breathing novel ever written, even opening on a dark and stormy night, during which sweet, virginal country girl Mercy-Ann Dunwoody, she of the rosy-cheeked, peasant-bloused variety, was ravished by the local squire which, according to the eaves-dropping Mr Phipps, was apparently par-for-the-course in those older, happier times. Even more predictably, as soon as she found herself with child - or in this case, triplets - Mercy-Ann Dunwoody was thrown out upon the cruel hard world to fend for herself.

'And what could the poor girl do to survive?' demanded Mrs Ballard. With her literary track record, I had more than a sneaking suspicion. She leaned closer, lowered her voice, and said:

'She was forced to become a *belle de nuit*, as I believe you people call them.'

Surprise, surprise. The career Mrs Ballard had decided upon for her heroine had obviously been chosen to allow its author ample opportunity to describe the sexual practices, peccadilloes and perversions of the period at great length. Which she duly did. And in graphic detail. By the time she was approaching the end of her sordid little saga, I was searching desperately for a way of escape. Thankfully, this came in the shape of Daphne and Deirdre, who whisked me off to their flat for a nightcap.

'So what d'you think?' Mrs Ballard called after me, as Daphne and Deirdre hustled me towards the front entrance.

'Not enough sex in it,' I called back over my shoulder. Well, I had to say something.

She was obviously delighted with my response: 'Well thank you!' She actually beamed: 'That's just what I thought!'

And she scuttled after us, presumably intent on applying pen to paper the moment she got home. Well, I thought, why not? It was a harmless, if totally futile part-time occupation and, unlike the unfortunate Mercy-Ann Dunwoody, it did keep her off the streets.

❧

On reaching my own apartment, an hour or so later, I was half-pleased, half-apprehensive, to see the incoming message light flashing on my answering machine. Geneviève's message was short and to the point. She was about to leave the city for a tour of the regions on an economic fact-finding mission and would be unable to contact me again for some considerable time. My depression at the news was only slightly alleviated by the warmth in her voice, when she said softly, finally:

'Au voir, chéri. Je t'aime. Je crois.'

That she loved me was encouraging. That she only thought she did was less so and for one lunatic moment, I actually began to toy with the idea of investigating the going rates for camels, goats and hashish, in the event of having to make a counter-offer for her services. I consoled myself with the old adage that a man supposedly chases a girl until she catches him. Let the chase commence, I thought, wistfully. And as soon as possible.

✧✧✧

The call from *Le Courrier's* travel editor came the following morning.

'A favour, Pierre,' he said: 'Could you possibly help an old friend of mine to find some reasonably-priced accommodation in London?'

It seemed that his free-lance financial journalist friend was about to be seconded to London by a French newspaper to write a series of articles comparing the financial and productivity forecasts of those countries that had adopted the euro and those that had yet to do so. The editor's friend needed to reside in London for at least the next six months and, as I had already been here for almost a year, the editor had (erroneously) assumed that I would, by now, be fully *au fait* with everything English, including the going rates for accommodation.

'It'll be his first time in London,' said the editor: 'And he doesn't want to get ripped off. We all know that as soon as the

English hear a foreign accent, the prices are automatically doubled.'

While I had yet to find that to be the case, I could hardly refuse my employer's cry for help in his friend's hour of need and I promised to do all I could to help him find a suitable flat or bed-sitter. The friend turned up on the Monday of the following week, with eight suitcases and a wife. Jacques Roussin seemed a pleasant enough man. Around 50, rotund of body with thinning hair, a permanently cheerful expression and a rather damp handshake. He allowed me to give his equally-rotund and equally-cheerful spouse a discreet peck on the cheek, before asking me if he could borrow a few English pounds to pay his taxi driver:

'I was sure I had enough, but the taxi-fares in London are *horribles*.'

Recalling the taxi-driving Constantin of last New Year's Eve, I had to agree with him and brought out my wallet.

'*Merci*. I'll let you have it back, of course, as soon as I've cashed some travellers' cheques.'

Later, over a cup of coffee in my apartment, while his wife was in the bathroom rebuilding her *visage*, I suggested we made a plan of action:

'First, what sort of area did you have in mind?'

A shrug: 'How would I know? It's my first time in London.' He gestured towards the window: 'Around here seems to be pleasant enough and I gather it's fairly convenient for the City of London - the financial quarter, I mean.'

'In that case, I suggest we do the rounds of the local letting agents.'

He nodded: 'That would seem to make sense.'

'But I warn you, accommodation around here is not cheap.'

He glanced around him: 'This place seems quite nice. One bedroom? Two?'

'Three. But don't ask me how much it would cost to rent on the open market. It's a company flat.'

'Ah,' he said: 'Still very nice.' Then after a pause: 'Three bedrooms, you said.'

'Yes.'

Suddenly, I didn't like the direction in which the conversation seemed to be heading, but remembering my promise to my editor, I couldn't ignore the inevitable question:

'Where will you be staying in the meantime?'

Another Gallic shrug and a lift of the hands: 'No idea. We thought you might know of somewhere. Y'know, somewhere not too expensive.'

My (albeit reluctant) offer to put them up for the night was gratefully accepted, though one week later he and his wife were still occupying the larger of the other two bedrooms while he and I trudged around the letting agents and inspected a wide variety of apartments. Unfortunately, none of them seemed to meet with his approval, being too small, too large, too expensive or too far from the shops/restaurants/transport. While I could understand his reluctance to pay through *le nez* for a six months' tenure, he did not appear to be short of money, as his wife spent most of her time flitting from shop to *boutique* in London's West End, returning at the end of the day with, as the ubiquitous Binkie had once put it, enough carrier bags to open her own department store.

On the evenings when I had to leave them alone in the flat while I assessed a London hotel or restaurant, Madame Roussin did cook the occasional meal - for herself and her husband - usually with ingredients she had discovered in my refrigerator or deep-freeze. They also seemed to approve of the now rapidly-diminishing wine cellar I had inherited from the late Antoine Didier, as evidenced by the number of empty wine and spirit bottles that had appeared over the past seven days. As, presumably, they had no wish to embarrass me by offering to replace them, they didn't. What was more, obviously due to a bout of temporary amnesia since his arrival, M. Roussin had yet to repay me the money I had loaned him the night they had arrived, in order to pay for their taxi.

In other words and not to put too fine a point on it, Monsieur and Madame Roussin were a pair of tight-fisted, free-loading *misères* who were using their friendship with my employer to abuse my hospitality for as long as they could get away with it. And unhappily, until they finally decided to move out, if ever, it seemed I had no way of making them leave, without alienating the one person who kept me in gainful employment.

❧

'They're very messy, your house-guests,' said actor-cleaner Maggie Turnbull, as she exchanged her slippers for her Doc Martens, while sipping her usual cup of black instant coffee: 'Their bedroom is a tip. None of my business, but how long are they staying?'

'I wish I knew,' I said gloomily: 'They're friends of my boss.'

'Oh, like that is it? Poor Mr LaPoste. You really do get lumbered, don't you?'

'Lumbered?'

'Taken advantage of. First pretty little *Mademoiselle de Ménerbes* and now these two. What are you going to do about it?'

'What can I do?'

She sighed: 'I've told you before, Pierre, there's always something to be done. Want me to think about it?'

'Would you?'

She would. And she did. For on my return from a week's tour of the Kent coast's hotels and restaurants, I found that Monsieur and Madame Roussin had packed their suitcases and carrier bags and migrated to rented accommodation in another part of London, which I later discovered to be a double bed-sitter in East Croydon, the nearest they could get to Central London at the price they were prepared to pay. Their note was short and to the point and, it seemed, written in some haste. It thanked me for my hospitality, assured me that they would say complimentary things about me when they next saw their friend and my employer and, almost unbelievably, apologised for not having repaid their borrowed cab-fare earlier, which was attached herewith.

'How on earth did you do it?' I asked Maggie, when she dropped in to see if they had gone.

She shrugged: 'I suddenly remembered a play I'd once been in. A fringe thing that played mostly to social misfits, pseudo-intellectuals and theatre-going masochists who were all into worthy plays of gloom, despair and despondency.'

'What part did you play?'

'Third leper.'

'Pardon?'

'That's what the play was about - a leper colony in biblical times. Not a lot of laughs, but it did give me an idea.'

'On, no,' I said: 'You didn't. Please say you didn't.'

'I didn't what?'

'Tell them you were a leper.'

197

Maggie looked at me in surprise: 'Of course I didn't. What sort of person d'you think I am? That would have been gross.' She still looked quite pleased with herself, however: 'No, I simply hinted that I'd once suffered from something along those lines. You know, something itchy with spots. *Like Beri-Beri. Yellow Jack.* Or *Moby Dick.*'

'*Moby Dick*?'

'I'm not quite sure what that is, either,' she admitted, cheerfully: 'But it does sound rather nasty, doesn't it?'

I looked at her, in astonishment: 'I can hardly believe you actually told them you had a virulent disease.'

'I didn't. That would have been a fib, wouldn't it? No. Like I said, I just sort of... floated the idea.'

'That's outrageous, Maggie. How could you?'

She grinned: 'With the greatest of ease.' She was quite unrepentant: 'I know it was a bit naughty of me, but I could see that they were the sort of people you wouldn't be able to shift with dynamite.' She adopted an expression of wide-eyed innocence: 'Naturally, I assured them there was no question of them catching anything and if they'd like me to make them a sandwich while I was there...' She gave a deep, rumbling laugh: 'You should have seen their faces. Especially when I sort of absent-mindedly started scratching myself. They were out of here like a stick of turkey-rhubarb.'

'Turkey-rhubarb?'

She sighed: 'You're doing it again, aren't you? Repeating everything I say.'

'Sorry.'

'If you must know, it's a stick of liquorice. Gives you the trots.' She gave another chuckle: 'You should have been here, Pierre. I could hardly stop myself from corpsing' - and before I could open my mouth – 'getting the giggles. But then,' she continued proudly: 'I'm a professional, aren't I?'

The wonderfully wicked Maggie Turnbull was more than that. She was my guardian angel and I prayed that one day she would meet the sort of life partner she so richly deserved.

November was about to tip over into December, happily without further mishap, but also, without any further communication from the fragrant Geneviève. Surely she had to be home for Christmas? While I accepted the fact that their Arab hosts were probably not all that *au fait* or even concerned with the religious and, it has to be said, commercial significance of December 25th to the Western world, I would have thought that the British Foreign Office would have insisted that the members of its trade mission be allowed to return home to celebrate Christmas with their families, no matter how important their trade mission happened to be.

Confident that the British Foreign Secretary, a family man himself, would do just that, I decided to telephone the Foreign Office and request the exact date of Geneviève's return. Which turned out to be a little more difficult than I'd anticipated.

Pierre LaPoste

DECEMBER

I T SNOWED IN DECEMBER. Not a lot, but enough to mantle the roofs and gardens of Muswell Hill with a Christmas-cardy promise of festive things to come. Not that there would be much to be festive about in the absence of Geneviève Tomlinson. My attempts to prise any information from the British Foreign Office about her present location and when I might expect her return to the UK, were met with deep suspicion. All the various Foreign Office officials to whom I had spoken on the telephone seemed to react with a sort of professional paranoia, the moment they heard my French accent. They had obviously convinced themselves that my request for information about a member of a British trade delegation had to be part of a dastardly French plot to send a competitive delegation, the moment they ascertained with whom the British were negotiating and for what.

I tried my hardest to convince them that this was a purely personal matter and that the lady in question was my *fiancée*, which they refused to believe, possibly because as yet, it wasn't true. But to no avail.

'Why don't you have a word with our local Member of

Parliament?' suggested Daphne: 'She might be able to find out for you.'

As they had promised, Daphne and Deirdre had dropped in for a coffee and also, presumably, to make sure I had not replaced Michelle with a Colette or a Mireille or even a Fifi, in Geneviève's absence.

'She's quite famous, this MP of ours,' said Daphne. Then to Deirdre: 'What's her name again?'

Deirdre wrinkled her brow: 'Can't think of it at the moment. Barbara something. A Mrs... er... what is it now? Sounds a bit French. Is it a Mrs Boche?'

'I thought that was German,' said Daphne.

Said Deirdre: 'That can't be right, then, can it? I'm sure she's not German. Hold on. It's on the tip of my tongue... dear, oh dear, oh lor. I'd forget my own head if it was loose. But anyway, Pierre. Everyone knows her.'

'Everyone,' agreed Daphne.

Apart from two ex *Nudes in a Lion's Cage*, it seemed.

Said Deirdre: 'We've never actually met her, but she can't be all bad. It seems that before she went into politics, she was one of us.'

'One of you?'

'A dancer. She was a Tiller girl. At the *London Palladium*.'

Said Daphne: 'That was Betty Boothroyd, you silly tart.' And to me: 'But why don't you go along to one of her surgeries in Crouch End?'

'She's a doctor, too?'

'No, Pierre,' said Deirdre patiently: 'Not that sort of surgery. The sort that gives advice to her constituents, not a dispensary for pills and potions.'

'But why should she help me?' I said: 'She's not my MP.

I'm a foreign national.'

Said Deirdre: 'As long as you live in Haringey, she's your MP. So why don't you run along to Middle Lane, tell her you're a close personal friend of Pierre Cardin, Sacha Distel and Bridget Bardot and see what her reaction is?'

At a guess, I thought, a look of total disbelief, followed by a loud horse laugh and a polite request to close the door quietly on my way out.

'Even so,' said Daphne, reading my thoughts: 'What have you got to lose?'

She did have a point. I was now desperately seeking straws at which to snatch and accordingly, that same weekend, I duly presented myself at the surgery of the Honourable Member for Hornsey and Wood Green (which encompassed Muswell Hill). She listened politely and patiently to what I had to say, made some notes, told me she'd make some enquiries and said that one of her staff would get back to me. And a few days later one did. The news was not encouraging. While the delegation hoped to return in time for Christmas, the negotiations were at such a delicate stage there was no guarantee that they would even be able to return by the end of the year. As promised, I reported this to Daphne and Deirdre.

'Not to worry,' said Daphne: 'You can spend Christmas with us.'

'Which reminds me,' said Deirdre: '*The Christmas Food and Crafts Fair* at Alexandra Palace is open. Lots of things to buy for Christmas presents. Want to come with us, Pierre?'

'Why not?' I said mournfully: 'I can drop in at the Garden Centre at the same time and buy myself a nice big packet of weedkiller.'

'Oh don't be such a wet lettuce,' said Daphne: 'I'm sure

Geneviève will be home sooner rather than later. And since we've been talking, the sun's gone over the yard-arm - if not in Muswell Hill, certainly in Bangkok. So what's your real poison - scotch, gin, brandy or vodka?'

By the end of the evening, it was all four.

When I awoke the following morning, I was not a well person. But a promise was a promise and I rose from my bed of pain, took a few aspirins and joined Daphne and Deirdre at their apartment prior to savouring the delights of the *Food and Crafts Fair* at Alexandra Palace. The walk through Springfield Avenue with a sprightly ex *danseuse* on each arm did much to help clear my head and raise my spirits. The air was crisp and bracing and I could already feel that indefinable spirit of Christmas beginning to permeate the crowds of shoppers walking towards the Palace.

As we made our way along the avenue, the twinkling lights from Christmas decorations were already very much in evidence. The bare branches of some front-garden trees were now intertwined with fairy lights and through many living room windows could be seen the wide variety of glittering decorations that draped the family Christmas trees. It was a pretty sight and I readily accepted Daphne's and Deirdre's invitation to help decorate their own tree. I did not know why they had obviously decided to adopt me for Christmas, but in the circumstances, I was extremely glad that they had.

'Oh look,' said Daphne as we entered the Palace main entrance: 'They've got an *Antiques Fair*, too.'

'Then keep well away, dear,' advised Deirdre: 'Or someone might make an offer for you.'

'I wish,' sighed Daphne: 'But more likely, I'd end up in the bargain basement.'

'Nonsense,' I said gallantly: 'If I wasn't spoken for, I'd snap you both up immediately.'

'Did you hear that, Daphne? How very sweet and how very French of you, Pierre. As Geneviève said, you're *tray genteel*.'

'And full of crap,' added Daphne: 'But we like it.'

She squeezed my arm affectionately and we went into the main hall. Shopping with *Les Girls* turned out to be quite an experience. At many of the various stalls, shoppers were invited to taste before buying, which Deirdre and Daphne did, with great enthusiasm, often requesting a second taste just to make sure. They moved slowly around the hall, starting with meat, fish and cheese savouries before finally ending up at those stalls offering cream pastries, biscuits and chocolate confectionery.

'Well that's lunch taken care of,' said Daphne, delicately brushing away a cake crumb from her carefully carmined lips.

Deirdre caught my amused look and said: 'She really means it, Pierre. Old habits die hard. If you'd been in *The Business* as long as we were, you'd never have passed up the chance of a free meal, either. Especially when you often didn't know where the next one was coming from.'

For a moment, she and Daphne were silent. I was later to learn that Deirdre's words had sparked off memories of less-than-happy times, when they would have gladly exchanged all the glitter and glamour of show business for a couple of the sample sausage rolls they'd just consumed. But as if to prove they were not merely a couple of cheap-skates, as the Americans say, they went around the hall for a second time, loading their sturdy shopping bags with many of the products they'd already tried and tested.

'Here, let me take those,' I said, when both women began to struggle under the weight of their purchases. They handed them over immediately.

'We thought you'd never ask,' said Daphne.

Said Deirdre: 'Why d'you think we asked you to come with us in the first place?' They both giggled: 'Now let's have a look at the arts and crafts.'

∝✼∾

There was a wide range from which to choose. Most of the leather goods were of good quality, as were the knitwear items, decorations, various types of flower vases, table mats, hand-carved wooden animals and assorted glassware. To my surprise, however, Daphne and Deirdre were immediately drawn to a small corner stall on which were displayed a bewildering array of what I believe our American cousins call *dreck* - from the German word for dirt or rubbish. With little whoops of joy, they pounced on what were to me revoltingly sentimental framed prints of fluffy little kittens playing with balls of wool, extremely garish mens' sweaters made from a coarse, hairy material apparently designed to give its wearer a permanent itch, plastic dipping ostriches that occasionally buried their beaks in a glass of water and a nausea-inducing range of liquid-filled table lamps that regularly regurgitated coloured oily bubbles.

I have to admit I was rather disappointed at their execrable taste when choosing what I presumed to be intended as Christmas presents for their friends and acquaintances. My expression of disapproval must have given me away, for as one, they burst into hoots of laughter.

'Hideous, aren't they?' chuckled Daphne.

'We buy this sort of junk every year,' said Deirdre: 'To give to people we don't particularly like. We stick them under our Christmas tree and hand them out at our annual drinks party.' She pointed to the regurgitating lamp: 'That's for Betty Ballard. To match the one we gave her last year.'

Said Daphne: 'The sweater's for Mr. Phipps - because he's such a scratchy old sod at the best of times.' She gave another little chuckle: 'You should see their faces when they open their presents. It's an entertainment in itself.'

'Malcolm Nesbitt's the biggest problem,' said Deirdre: 'No matter how appalling the present, he always seems to love it.'

Deirdre nodded: 'This year, we must find something really crummy for him. Something even he would hate at first sight.'

She looked around the hall, then pointed towards a stall selling T-shirts, with a while-you-wait printing service that offered to add the words of your choice.

'Hey,' said Deirdre: 'How about a shirt with something really vulgar on the front?'

'Such as?' said Daphne.

'I dunno - hold on - how about *Chiropodists Do It On Their Feet*?'

Daphne shook her head: 'Not vulgar enough. And anyway, he probably wouldn't get the joke. And if he did, he'd just wear the shirt back to front, under that awful paisley pullover of his.'

The predictably surreal debate continued all the way back to Arcadia Court and after depositing their purchases at their apartment, I returned to my flat wondering what sort of present the two wicked women had in mind for me at their annual drinks party on Christmas Eve. Knowing them, I told myself to be prepared for anything, no matter how bizarre. In the event, I was taken completely by surprise.

≈≈≈

The telephone rang as I entered my doorway.

'Good news, Pierre,' said the travel editor of *Le Courrier de Paris*. 'My friends the Roussins spoke very highly of you and as you've obviously done more than your share of standing-in for Antoine Didier and putting up with the English weather, I've found you a replacement. A young journalist who can't wait to savour the delights of *la cuisine anglaise*.' He chuckled: 'Though to be honest, I think what he really wants to experience is the allegedly knee-jerk reaction of any *jeune fille anglaise* to the sound of a French accent. So welcome home, Pierre.'

For a moment, I couldn't quite take it in. By now, I was so used to my Anglicised way of life, the thought of having re-adjust to living and working in Provence once again was, somewhat to my surprise, strangely unappealing.

'You still there, Pierre?'

'Oh. Yes. Course. Thanks for the call.'

'Not at all. See you in the New Year.'

But as soon as I put the phone down, I knew in my heart I did not wish to go back to France on a permanent basis. I liked Provence. I liked Ménerbes. But I had now also acquired a certain affection for life and living in Muswell Hill. Certainly, as my editor had said, it wasn't because of the weather and not because it happened to be the place where I had met the object of my desire. But because of the people. Their warmth, their irascibility, their friendship, their honesty, their politeness, their rudeness, their eccentricities but, above all, (and forgive me, Napoleon Bonaparte) their Englishness.

Warts and all, as Oliver Cromwell might have said.

My year in Muswell Hill had, to my own utter astonishment, succeeded in exorcising my deeply-rooted prejudices and preconceptions about the English and their way of life. Well, some of them. And I could only hope that one day, the Betty Ballards of this world would begin to feel the same way about the French. But as Mr. Phipps might well say - fat chance. And sadly, he'd probably be right.

I wondered how my editor would react if I returned his call and requested him to allow me to spend another year in Muswell Hill. After, presumably, the sound of a jaw being well and truly dropped at my inconceivable desire to eschew the joys of rural Lubéron for a busy, fume-laden North London suburb, would he agree to my request? But as I reached for the phone, I realised that the whole question was entirely academic, until the lovely, pouting Geneviève Tomlinson had decided to make an honest man of me. Or not, as the case may be. If her decision was the one I so fervently hoped for, then asking her to leave Muswell Hill to live in Ménerbes would be quite out of the question.

I could hardly expect a "woman of some importance," as most English males grudgingly call a high-flying female, to give up her job at the British Foreign Office, sell her apartment and move back to France with me on a permanent basis. It would be too much to ask. I replaced the phone and went to bed.

෨෬෯

Daphne's and Deirdre's apparent determination to keep me fully occupied during my leisure hours until Geneviève's return was further evidenced by an invitation to accompany them to the local Community Centre to see a performance of the annual Christmas pantomime. I'd heard of pantomimes, of course, but I'd never seen one and, to be honest, didn't know quite what to expect.

Les Girls' on-going support for anything theatrical - from actor-cleaners to touring thespians - resulted in us boarding a number 134 bus the following evening and alighting at the local Community Centre, which turned out to be a converted church where a variety of activities took place. According to Daphne and Deirdre, these included art classes with live artists' models, which had resulted in many local males suddenly discovering an irresistible urge to paint, senior citizens' kung-fu classes, creative courses in street graffiti, geriatric line-dancing nights, local rock bands, pottery classes and theatrical groups - both amateur and professional - and, on this occasion, a professional production of *Mother Goose*.

The annual Christmas pantomime, I was to discover, is an English phenomenon. Traditionally and quite incomprehensibly, the male leading role is played by a statuesque female, with magnificent thighs that are required to be slapped at regular intervals.

Often in the guise of characters such as Dick Whittington - he of Highgate Hill hospital fame - or Aladdin or Prince Charming, the bosomy hero lays siege to the affections of the young and winsome heroine who, somewhat surprisingly in the circumstances, is actually played by a young and winsome female. With an equal perversity, the female comedy roles (such as the Ugly Sisters) are invariably played by men wearing garish multi-coloured underwear and inflated bosoms.

Again according to Deirdre and Daphne, during the course of the performance *sous-entendus* abounded, most of them hopefully going over the heads of the children in the audience:

'Tis after twelve of the clock and still no Dick,' bewails the presumably frustrated heroine, until the dilatory Dick accompanied by his/her cat, bounds on to the stage, slaps his/her thighs, turns to his/her feline co-star and declares, in tortured rhyming panto-speak:

'Hold hard, Puss, hold hard, I say. You don't see a maid like her every day.'

This year, Mother Goose was played by an ex television quiz-show host called Billy Beverage, whose career had seemingly been on the decline for some considerable time. Perhaps predictably, Daphne and Deirdre felt he needed all the support he could get.

'After all,' said Daphne: 'It wasn't really his fault.'

'What wasn't?' I asked, as we walked from the bus stop to the Community Centre.

It seemed that when appearing as a guest artiste on a well-known children's television show called *Blue Peter*, unaware that the programme was going out live, he had jokingly posed with a banana and two tangerines in front of the cameras and said:

'And here's one I had earlier."

Immediately, countless juvenile viewers had dived for the fruit bowl and proudly presented their parents with facsimiles of his multi-coloured erection. And from that moment on he had, in television terms, become one of Maggie Turnbull's theatrical lepers and reduced to touring in third-rate pantomimes produced on a shoe-string budget. Which probably explained why, after the curtain had gone up, Mother Goose was mostly played in front of a second-hand painted backcloth, depicting a village glade outside the city of Old Peking. Not that ancient China played any part in the story:

'A left-over from an amateur production of *Chu-Chin-Chow*,' whispered Deirdre, by way of explanation.

By the look of him, Mother Goose was not a happy man. Plump, middle-aged and prematurely balding, Bobby Beverage did not appear to have much going for him - apart from his dolefully comic features which, according to Daphne, had once been compared to a bag of walnuts.

It was a Saturday night and with no school in the morning, there was a heavy preponderance of unruly seven, eight and nine year olds in the audience. The show began when Mother Goose strode out on to the stage, driving a fat, ungainly goose before her. She gave a little twirl of her multi-coloured petticoats, disclosing the obligatory pink bloomers beneath, then smiled, curtsied and waited for the traditional round of applause at her first appearance. As a half-hearted ripple echoed around the theatre, the smile slipped into a rictal grimace and she turned quickly towards the goose, pointing imperiously at the imitation nesting box.

The vertically-challenged midget inside the moulting costume gave a grunt and a groan and laid a golden egg stage centre. The adults in the audience laughed dutifully. Their offspring merely jeered. Presumably reared from infancy on a diet of video nasties and questionable images on the internet, they'd seen it all before. Pantomimes were boring. Especially this one. And when could they go home, switch on the computer and decapitate a few aliens?

As the jeers increased, interspersed with ingenious suggestions as to what Mother Goose might do with her egg, Bobby Beverage picked it up and held it towards the audience with a forced smile: 'Who'd like to take home Goosey-Goosey-Gander's magic egg? The first little boy or girl to come up on to the - '

Before he could finish his sentence, the front rows erupted into a sea of shouting, struggling seven, eight and nine year olds, all striving to be the first to clamber on to the stage. It was quite obvious that none of them really coveted the supposedly-magical polystyrene egg, but any diversion had to be an improvement on having to sit watching a turgid story about a boring old woman and her scruffy-looking goose who, for reasons that had never been explained, kept ending up in China.

'Well?' asked Deirdre as we left the theatre and headed for the bus stop: 'Did you enjoy it?'

'It was quite an experience,' I said truthfully: 'The audience in particular. Such juvenile... exuberance.'

'Par for the course for a production like this,' said Deirdre.

'All part of the fun.' said Daphne.

And so ended my introduction to the traditional English Christmas pantomime and I idly wondered why our own famous *Comédie Française* didn't produce something similar. But only for a moment. They'd probably seen what happens at an English pantomime and had decided to stick with Molière.

The Carol Singers came early that December. The first inkling I had of their presence was the sound of four reedy voices, one of them completely out of tune with the others, singing the first few lines of *Away in a Manger* on the other side of my front door:

'Away in a Manger,
No crib for a Bed,
Little Lord Jesus,
Lay down his Sweet Head.'

The voices stopped as abruptly as they had begun then a moment later, the doorbell chimed, long and loud. I opened the door to find three scowling, rather scruffy small boys aged between nine and twelve and an even smaller and scruffier little girl standing there, with their hands held out, palms upwards.

'Merry Christmas,' said the marginally taller of the quartet.

'Merry Christmas to you, too,' I said politely, determined to prove to them I was not a soft touch.

There was a long silence, then by way of explanation the little girl said: 'We sung you a Christmas Carol.'

'Only a bit of one,' I pointed out.

'We don't know the rest of it,' said the middle one: 'But we'll give you a bit of *My Old Man's a Dustman*, if you like.'

And before I could stop them, that's what they did. At the tops of their voices. It was excruciating and I quickly pressed some small change into their hands before retreating hastily back inside my apartment, furious with myself for allowing them to vocally blackmail me into meeting their demands, as they had obviously intended. The sound of their voices continued for some time outside other apartments down the corridor, followed by the slamming of doors as the diminutive wassail-singing quartet extorted similar pay-offs from most of the other residents.

When I recounted my experience to Daphne and Deirdre over coffee the following morning, they merely chuckled.

'They sound like the Bellamy children from down the road,' said Daphne.

'Right little buggers they are too,' said Deirdre: 'Especially on trick-a-treat nights. Betty Ballard told them to hop it or else, so they dropped some doggie-do through her letter box.'

'You can't help but feel sorry for them, though,' said Daphne: 'What with their father in the Pentonville pokey and their mother trying to bring them up on her own, they don't have much of a life.'

Said Deirdre: 'That's why we always make sure they get something in their Christmas stockings. They don't know it's us, of course, but at least we make sure they don't feel left out.'

All my anger at the Bellamy children evaporated in an instant and not for the first time, I was touched by the kindness and understanding of the two ex *Danseuses Exotiques* for those less fortunate than themselves. What a tragedy, I thought, that they were never able to have children of their own. They would have made remarkable mothers.

❧

'You'll have to hurry up if you want a ticket,' said Mr Phipps, as we walked along the Broadway: 'They're going very fast.'

'A ticket for what?'

'I thought I'd mentioned it, but I obviously didn't. It's for a day-trip to Calais. One of the local travel agencies organises it. They do it every year.'

'Why should I want to go to Calais?'

He looked at me in surprise: 'To do your Christmas shopping, of course. At a hypermarket. Much cheaper than here. Fags, beer, wines and spirits. Being French, I thought you would have known that.'

I did know it, of course. I just hadn't given it much thought. For one thing, I didn't smoke. For another, thanks to the abrupt departure of the Roussins, there was still enough left over from the late Antoine Didier's stock of wines and spirits to see me comfortably through the seasonal festivities. Mr Phipps paused and pointed towards the travel agency on the other side of the Broadway.

'That's where you buy them. The tickets. We go by coach to Folkestone, drive on to the Euro-whatsit and half-an-hour later, we're filling our trolleys with enough booze to float a battleship.'

'Yes, well, the thing is, Mr Phipps - '

'Oh come on. It's a day out and it'll be useful having a genuine French bloke in the party.' And echoing the reverse of my travel editor's sentiments, almost word for word: 'Everyone knows that as soon as they hear an English accent, the French double their prices.'

A bit difficult at a hypermarket, I would have thought but, like he said, it would be a day out. And any suggestion of how to pass the hours until Geneviève's return was more than welcome.

Two days later, at eight o'clock on a cold and windy December morning, members of Mr Phipps' little party gathered outside the travel agents to wait the arrival of the motor coach from the nearby transport company.

The party consisted of Mr Phipps' pub-quiz team, including the woodwork-teaching Arthur, his fingers still festooned with blood-stained bandages, the Encyclopedia Britannica-reading Enid, football-genius Shane, plus Enid's earnest, bespectacled teenage daughter and her equally earnest and equally bespectacled boyfriend, who on the arrival of the coach, immediately dived for a twin rear seat and went into an amorous clinch that lasted all the way to Calais, without once coming up for air.

The other passengers I did not know. Neither, it seemed, did Mr Phipps' party, but that didn't stop them enthusiastically joining in the sing-song that began the moment the bus got under way and, like the teenagers' clinch, lasted all the way to Calais.

This peculiar English compunction to burst into song when travelling along the highways and byways of their sceptered isle was strangely endearing. On occasions such as this, the so-called reserved English seem to cast all their inhibitions aside to sing interminable renditions of such traditional airs as *One Man Went to Mow, Ten Green Bottles* and, somewhat incongruously, *You Ain't Nothing but a Hound Dog*. To my surprise, I found myself joining in and by the time we reached Calais, like many of the others, my voice had been reduced to a husky croak which, coupled with my French accent, made me sound like a cut-price Maurice Chevalier. Much to my embarrassment, this resulted in an arch smile plus a flutter of the eyelashes from an unaccompanied middle-aged lady from across the aisle, which made me resolve to change my seat for the return journey.

Mr Phipps' party descended upon the hypermarket like a swarm of hungry locusts and as I looked at their packed trolleys, I couldn't help wondering how all their crates of wines, spirits and beer could all be carried in the luggage compartment of the motor coach without seriously damaging the suspension. But the coach-driver had been there before and to my surprise, all was safely stowed away in a matter of minutes, ready for the journey home. But first, Mr Phipps announced, came luncheon and we followed him to the pre-booked *café* just off the main boulevard, where, somewhat predictably, he ordered a hamburger, chips and peas and Shane settled down to steak, eggs and chips. Only Enid, Arthur and I took advantage of our day in Calais to sample the local cuisine with *moules marinière* followed by *crême brulée*, both of which were extremely acceptable. Enid's daughter and her boyfriend did not appear to be hungry, both simply munching on a bread roll while staring soulfully into each others eyes, across the table.

We arrived back in Muswell Hill at dusk and went our separate ways. All in all, it had been an enjoyable journey and in my case, had solved the difficult problem of what to give Daphne and Deirdre for Christmas. As I wandered down the aisles of the hypermarket, the *euro* had again suddenly dropped. What else should I give to two glamorous and exotique little ladies who had a fondness for *La Belle Vie*, but a case of rather good champagne? I was not to know that their present to me would prove to be even more *exotique*.

Les Girls' Christmas drinks party always took place on Christmas Eve, when presents would be exchanged and the traditional mulled wine consumed in large quantities. Mince pies would abound and chestnuts would be roasted on an open fire - or at least, in a gas oven, Regulo 8.

Daphne's and Deirdre's annual party was certainly a popular social event for the residents of Arcadia Court and when I arrived, staggering under the weight of 12 bottles of champagne, the party was just beginning. Most of the residents were there, including a sullen little Alice who bared her teeth whenever anyone came too near to her permanent berth in Mrs Nesbitt's lap. Even the socially reclusive literary agent Mr Sharples turned up with the hint of a smile and a signed copy of the fabled Phyllis Dixie's Autobiography, which chartered the chequered career of England's first great *poseur érotique*, much to the delight of the joint hostesses.

Indeed, everyone bought a gift of one kind or another and everyone received one. Betty Ballard's face on opening her present was, as Daphne had forecast, a picture of dismay, followed by a totally spurious smile and an even more insincere expression of gratitude. Mr Phipps' quite grisly sweater was received with an equal lack of enthusiasm. This year, it seemed that Deidre and Daphne had finally succeeded in choosing a present that even Malcolm Nesbitt would have no use for.

'Very nice,' he said bemusedly, as he took off the wrapping to reveal a book entitled *Ernest J. Leadbetter, Father of Modern Sewage Disposal. An Appreciation.*

'It's quite a rare book,' said Deirdre: 'Not many of them about.'

'I wonder why?' muttered Mrs Ballard, in the background.

'We saw it on the antique book stall at the *Food and Crafts Fair* and thought it might interest you,' said Daphne, quite dead-pan: 'It tells you everything you wanted to know about effluence, but were too shy to ask.'

Malcolm nodded blankly. The two women looked at each other and smiled, as if metaphorically punching the air in triumph. The present-swapping continued. Mr Sharples surreptitiously slipped me a copy of a booklet published by the L.A.A., which turned out to be an acronym for the *Literary Agents Association*. The booklet, despite its somewhat ambiguous title: *'Who Needs A Literary Agent?'* was presumably intended to promote their services, for

Sharples then lowered his voice, mumbled 'I think we should talk' and disappeared in the direction of the mulled wine.

Even though Daphne and Deirdre had once confided to me that little Alice's constant yapping drove them to distraction, there was still a present for her - a rubber bone which squeaked as she bit it and obviously infuriated her, which perhaps is what the women had intended. Although the party was in its very early stages, I was one of the first to receive a present. Daphne turned to Deirdre and said:

'Get Pierre his present, will you, dear? It's in the guest-room.' To me, she said: 'It was too big to put under the tree.'

Said Deirdre: 'Would you mind getting it yourself, Pierre? I've got to take the mince pies out of the oven.'

'Not at all,' I said, wondering what on earth could be so big that it couldn't be placed under the tree. I walked down the inner corridor and opened the door to the guest-room.

Geneviève Tomlinson was sitting in the bedside chair, holding two empty glasses and a bottle of champagne.

'*Bonjour, Matelot,*' she said: '*Joyeux Noël, et voulez-vous coucher avec moi ce soir?*'

❧

'There's still time for you to make a run for it,' she said the following morning: 'Not that you'd get very far. You're all mine, Pierre LaPoste. And vice-versa.'

It seemed that Daphne and Deirdre had seen her climbing out of the taxi just a few minutes before the start of the party and had arranged the whole thing.

'There's just one problem,' I said: 'Where are we going to live? Here or there?'

'Here and there. As it's only seven hours from Waterloo to Aix, we can spend the winter in Muswell Hill and the summer in Ménerbes. How does that grab you?'

It grabbed me exceedingly well, as I was sure it would grab my editor.

Christmas passed and New Year's Eve arrived on schedule. As we went to bed, we heard the sound of the St. James Church clock at the end of the Broadway striking midnight. We kissed. My Year in Muswell Hill was *complete*.

In every possible way.

FIN